KINDLINGS

By Ian Macpherson

KINDLINGS

Outlines and Sermon Starters

Ian Macpherson

FLEMING H. REVELL COMPANY
OLD TAPPAN, NEW JERSEY

Copyright © 1969 by Fleming H. Revell Company
All Rights Reserved
Library of Congress Catalog Card Number: 72–77481
Printed in the United States of America

PREFACE

In *Personal Encounters,* a book of random reminiscences of a long and successful ministry in the Church of Scotland, Dr. D.P. Thomson tells of some memorable hours spent in 1928 with Dr. George H. Morrison, the well-known preacher of the Wellington Church, Glasgow.

"As we sat by the study fireside in my manse," Dr. Thomson recalls, "he asked me to go over some of the outlines I had been preparing for the years ahead, for my own use and for the use of others. 'Thank you, my boy,' he said, as he rose to go to bed, 'you have given me my Sunday evening sermons for next winter.' "

On which Dr. Thomson comments: "I knew well what he meant, and I only wish it had been possible to see or hear what he made of them. All he needed was a line of thought, at once clear and compelling. His genius could accomplish the rest" (*Op. cit.,* Crieff, Scotland: The Research Unit, 1967, p. 73).

If the mind of such a master of the pulpit as Morrison benefited from homiletic priming of that kind, may not those of other ministers also find stimulus and inspiration in preaching points?

This book is published in the hope and with the prayer that they will!

Ian Macpherson,
Glasgow

CONTENTS

8

KINDLINGS

IDOLS

You turned to God from idols, to serve a living and true God. 1 Thessalonians 1:9

Modern man has left the grosser forms of idolatry forever behind. He no longer bows down to sticks and stones, nor worships the works of his own hands. You will not find the educated human of today falling down before Mars or Venus, Thor or Odin. Nevertheless, man never really turns from idols until he turns to the living God. That is the inevitable process of sublimation by which idolatrous practices are replaced by true worship.

Idols may be said to fall into three categories.

1. **There are material idols.**

Billy Graham writes, "Too many of today's professing Christians would give up going to church before they would give up getting a new refrigerator. Given the choice between making the down payment on a new car, or contributing to the cost of building a new Sunday School, it is easy to guess what the decision of many would be. Thousands of so-called Christians are putting money, and the things that make up our high standard of living, ahead of the teaching of Christ. We can save towards a new home, or a bigger television set, but we feel that we can no longer afford to tithe. This is idolatry." (Quoted by Hugh Robert Macdonald, *On Top of the World,* London, Marshall, Morgan & Scott, 1965, p. 139.)

2. There are mental idols.

William Temple, Archbishop of Canterbury, once neatly put it, "A false mental image is as much an idol as a false metal image."

3. There are moral idols.

We are all familiar with the names of the idols of stage and stadium, the stars of the worlds of entertainment and of sport. Billy Graham has turned from such idols. "Jesus is my idol," he says.

What Religion Really Is

Religion that is pure and undefiled before God and the Father is this: to visit orphans and widows in their affliction, and to keep oneself unstained from the world. James 1:27

At a great meeting in London many years ago one of the speakers took three points as the pegs of his address.

1. Religion is first an experience and afterwards a creed.

A man may eat and benefit by his dinner who never looked inside a cookbook, and who knows nothing whatever of the physiological processes involved in eating and drinking.

It is related that a preacher, once famous for his quaintness in the pulpit, on one occasion quoted Paul's words, "Great is the mystery of godliness." "Seeking to make plain that whatever theoretical difficulties there might be about religion, these were no sufficient reason why a man should not enjoy the practical good of it, he seized the glass of water that stood in the pulpit by his side. "Great is the mystery of water!" he cried, and launched into a talk about oxygen and hydrogen, the proportions in which they combine to produce water, and so forth. "Great is the mystery of water. Nevertheless," he added with a merry twinkle, and suiting the action to the word, "we'll take a drink!"

2. **Religion is primarily an inspiration rather than a restraint.**

All Christ's restraints, if we understand them right, are inspirations. When He says, "Give up," it is because He is about to say, "Receive ye."

3. **Religion is a program for the present life as well as an insurance for the future.**

It is always easy, and just now it is rather popular, to sneer at what we call *other-worldliness*. Nevertheless, other-worldliness has a very large place in the New Testament. But nothing is more vain than to suppose that any religion will ever speak with authority to the heart and conscience of man, which has no outlook into the eternal world. Secular gospels may secure the suffrage of the hour, but there can be no lasting home for the soul of man in any faith which is silent about the future.

(George Jackson, *A Young Man's Religion*, London, Hodder & Stoughton, 1906, p. 103 ff.)

THE CHALLENGE OF CHANGE

If any one is in Christ, he is a new creation; the old has passed away, behold, the new has come.
2 Corinthians 5:17

For all of us, or nearly all, there is a charm in change. In one way or another most of us would like to be different from what we are. One man is reported to have said, so satisfied was he with the manner in which God had made him, that, had he had a hand in the process, he would not have wished to alter it in the slightest degree. He was surely the exception, not the rule. Most of us want to be changed.

We see this illustrated sometimes in rather amusing ways. American and European ladies, for instance, spend a fortune on having their hair permanently waved, while African ladies spend a fortune on having theirs straightened! Not long ago I saw a white woman applying suntan lotion to her skin with a view to making herself brown, and a few minutes later I met an Indian lady who had powdered her face so liberally that it seemed as if she had fallen into a flour barrel! In a magazine the other day, I noticed on one page an advertisement for a certain brand of slimming tablets, and on the next page an advertisement for some patent preparation guaranteed to help one to put weight on!

Yes, in one direction or another most of us want to be changed. But do we want to be changed in the most radical fashion of all, changed as only Christ can change us?

John Wesley's favorite text assures us of the possibility. "If any one is in Christ, he is a new creation; the old has passed away, behold, the new has come" (2 Corinthians 5:17).

1. The new creature.

Creation, according to the old definition, is the bringing of something out of nothing. As Luther pointed out, nothingness is a prerequisite to creativity. God can make nothing of us until we make nothing of ourselves. But when, in humble penitence, we recognize our own utter nothingness, God can make something of us. "Therefore, if any man be in Christ, he is a new creature" (2 Corinthians 5:17, KJV).

2. The new nature.

"If any one is in Christ." Preaching once at a Pan-Presbyterian Conference in Edinburgh, the saintly Dr. Andrew Murray, of South Africa, took as his text Ephesians 4:24: "Put on the new nature, created after the likeness of God in true righteousness and holiness." The special point he made was that everything that God has created, He has created for some specific purpose and has provided it with facilities to fulfil its function. Thus God has created the birds to fly and has furnished them with wings; He has created the fishes to swim and He has equipped them with fins; and He has created the

Christian to do good works and has given him super-
natural power to do them. Just as it is the nature of the
bird to fly and of the fishes to swim, so it is the nature of
the Christian, a new nature imparted to him at regenera-
tion, to live a holy life.

3. The new future.

"Old things have passed away; behold, all things are
become new" (2 Corinthians 5:17, KJV).

The older one grows the more important for one becomes the future. More and more, one wants to know
where one is going and is not content simply to take
one's pleasure as it comes and where one finds it. The
last things become for us the first things, and the end
alone can give meaning and worth to the journey. Only
the Christian can thrill to the thought of the future.

CHANGING THE SIGNPOSTS

*Your ears shall hear a word behind you, saying:
"This is the way, walk in it," when you turn to
the right or when you turn to the left.* Isaiah
30:21

Professor G. N. M. Collins tells how, during a recent
visit to John o' Groats, the northern tip of Scotland, he
came across an enterprising commercial photographer who
had erected a signpost, "as near the most northerly part
of the Scottish mainland as he could select for his purpose. The direction arms were detached, but he had a

considerable selection of these at hand, and set them up as his customers might require."

While the professor looked on, a family from London posed for a photograph. The appropriate direction arm was set in position, giving the mileage from John o' Groats, and then the picture was taken—then Birmingham, then the town of Kirkwall in the Orkneys.

The photographer left his sign unattended for a time; and, during his absence, two roguish youths fixed the direction arm the wrong way—Kirkwall was indicated at some point away in the south, while London was located somewhere on the way to the North Pole!

That is a parable of what has happened in modern life. Let us think of some of the false directions now being popularly given. People are told:

1. **That the crooked road leads to prosperity.**

2. **That the broad road leads to happiness.**

3. **That the low road leads to self-fulfilment.**

But the only road worth travelling on is the highway spoken of in Isaiah 35:8-10:

> And a highway shall be there,
> and it shall be called the Holy Way;
> the unclean shall not pass over it,
> and fools shall not err therein.
> No lion shall be there,
> nor shall any ravenous beast come up on it;
> they shall not be found there,
> but the redeemed shall walk there.

And the ransomed of the Lord shall return,
and come to Zion with singing;
everlasting joy shall be upon their heads;
they shall obtain joy and gladness,
and sorrow and sighing shall flee away.

How Christ Makes Life Worthwhile

To live is Christ. Philippians 1:21

Is life worth living? Ask the doctor. "That," he will
tell you, "depends on the *liver.* It is all a matter of the
proper functioning of physical processes." Is life worth
living? Ask the economist. "That," he will reply, "depends on the *living.* It is entirely contingent upon social
conditions." Is life worth living? Ask the Christian. "That,"
he will answer, "depends on the *life.* Ultimately, no life
is worth living which is not rightly related to God through
Jesus Christ."

The truth of that statement is being dramatically illustrated by what is happening today in certain sections
of the student population. According to official reports,
they are committing suicide at an alarming rate. Now this
is not because there is anything wrong with their livers.
In nearly every one of them that delicate organ is working
perfectly. Nor is it because their living conditions are
poor. On the contrary, to use an overworked modern
phrase, they never had it so good. Yet apparently thousands of them would rather be extinct than extant. Before
they come to the end of their college course, they take a

short cut out of existence. For them life is not worth living.

Yet Paul found it so, though he suffered from a painful affliction which he called his "thorn in the flesh" and though he spent quite a lot of his time in a Roman prison. "To live is Christ," he cried.

You, too, can know through Christ that life is worth living. I want to address you on the subject of how Christ makes life worthwhile.

There are five ways in which He does it, and I propose to pass them in rapid review. Christ makes life worth living for you because: 1. He gives you a conscience you can live with; 2. a creed you can live by; 3. a cause you can live for; 4. a company you can live in; and 5. a consummation you can live towards.

1. **A conscience you can live with.**
   a. Some contrive to live with their consciences because they have chloroformed them. "Take away the alarmed conscience," cried Soren Kierkegaard, "and you may as well close our churches."
   b. Some cannot live with their consciences because they are condemnatory. Do you remember the haunting lines of Charles William Stubbs?

I sat alone with my conscience
 In a place where time had ceased,
And we talked of my former living
 In a land where the years increased.

The ghosts of forgotten actions
 Came floating before my sight,

And the things that I thought were dead things
  Were alive with a terrible might;

And I know of the future Judgment,
  How dreadful so'er it be,
To sit alone with my conscience
  Will be judgment enough for me.

    c. Some can live with their consciences because they
    have been purified and pacified by the blood of
    Christ.
    "How much more shall the blood of Christ, who
    through the eternal Spirit offered Himself with-
    out blemish to God, purify your conscience from
    dead works to serve the living God" (Hebrews
    9:14).

2. A creed you can live by.

"It is faith in something," wrote Oliver Wendell Holmes,
"that makes life worth living."

I remember walking one wild winter's day along a
street in the university town of Aberystwyth on the west
coast of Wales. A terrific gale was blowing and in front of
me, battling with it like myself, was a man who, on
reaching a certain point on the road, fumbled in his
pockets and produced a key. Then, approaching a house
by the wayside, he inserted the key in the front door
and passed at one step through the open door into the
welcoming warmth of the interior. It was the name of
the house that fascinated me, and which turned a very
ordinary everyday happening into a parable. The name
was *Credo*, Latin for *I Believe*.

The man who, amid the secularist blizzard of our time, can say *that* concerning the Christian faith has in truth a shelter in which he can find security and repose.

3. A cause you can live for.

"I am not satisfied to live," wrote W. E. Sangster as a lad; "I want something to live for."

Thomas Guthrie, the great Scottish preacher and philanthropist, once nearly proved himself a poet too. It was when he penned these lines:

> I live for those around me,
>   For those who love me true,
> For the heaven whose smile has found me
>   And awaits my spirit too:
> For the wrong that needs resistance,
> For the cause that lacks assistance,
> For the future in the distance
>   And the good that I can do.

4. A company you can live in.

Not long ago I visited a delinquent teen-ager in a Scottish Remand Home. He had been convicted on a serious charge and was in for a fairly long stretch. I got into conversation with the governor about him. "He's not a bad lad really," said the governor. "But the trouble is— he's easily led and had got into bad company. While in here, he's all right. He is perfectly docile and tractable, but once out, I'm afraid he'll get back to the gang he goes around with, and then it will be only a matter of time until he commits another, and perhaps an even graver, crime."

How important is good company to Christian youth!
The best company in the world is the church of Christ.

5. A consummation you can live towards.

"The true end of life," declared William Penn, "is to
know the life that never ends."

IF I WERE GOD

Whom makest thou thyself? John 8:53 KJV

Who do you make yourself out to be? That is what
Christ's critics meant. They thought He was putting on
airs, giving Himself graces, and professing to be greater
than the father of the Hebrew race himself. Little though
they dreamt it, the thing was true. In the sense that He
was the self-originating God, He had made Himself, and
He was infinitely greater than any other being who ever
walked this earth.

Nevertheless, people *do* sometimes make themselves
out to be other and greater than they are. They do have
illusions of grandeur. And the sanest of us has at times
asked himself the question: "What would I do if I
were God?"

Let us see how four representative persons answered
that inquiry.

1. "If I were God, I'd be angry."

That is what Martin Luther said. "If I were
God," he declared, "and the world had treated

24

me as it has treated Him, I'd kick the wretched thing to pieces."

A recent writer in *The Evangelical Beacon* reacted in the same way. He wrote:

> If I were God
> And man made a mire
> Of things: war, hatred,
> Murder, lust, cobwebs
> Of infamy, entangling
> The heart and soul,
> I would sweep him
> To one side and start anew.
> (I think I would.)
> If I did this,
> Would I be God?

2. "If I were God, I'd be brokenhearted."

That is what Johann Wolfgang von Goethe said. "If I were God," he averred, "the woes of the world would break my heart."

William Temple, Archbishop of Canterbury, observed: "Men say, 'There cannot be a God of love, because, if there were and He looked upon this world, His heart would break.' The Church points to the Cross, and says: 'His heart *does* break!' "

3. "If I were God, I'd be merciful."

That is what Martin Elginbrodde is made to say. We all remember the odd old epitaph:

Here lie I, Martin Elginbrodde;
Have mercy o' my soul, Lord God,
As I wad do, were I Lord God,
An' ye were Martin Elginbrodde.

4. **"If I were God, I'd be proud."**
   That is what A. A. Milne said. Into the mouth
   of one of the characters in his play *The Truth
   About Blayds* he puts the words: "If I were God,
   I'd be very proud of man."

THE CLOTHING OF THE SPIRIT

*Stay in the city, until you are clothed with power
from on high.* Luke 24:49

Wait till you are clothed with power! Clothed! That
is a vivid verb. The Greek word for clothing is *enduma,*
a term from which we get our English word *endue.* So
it is no wonder that the translators of the *King James
Version* took advantage of this linguistic link and rendered
the text: "Tarry . . . until ye be endued with power." But
the word *clothed* is stronger, more striking. "Stay . . . until
you are clothed with power."

1. Clothing is for concealment.

The man who is clothed with the Spirit is not an
exhibitionist. "The Holy Spirit is the only real power for
service. Why have we not this power? Because we are not
willing to be made invisible by the investiture," explains
Alexander Maclaren.

Rock of Ages, cleft for me,
Let me hide myself in Thee . . .
Naked, come to Thee for dress.

Augustus Toplady

2. Clothing is for warmth.

Do you know the balancings of the
    clouds,
  the wondrous works of him who
    is perfect in knowledge,
you whose garments are hot
  when the earth is still because of
    the south wind?

(Job 37:16, 17).

3. Clothing is for identification.

It marks the distinction of sex—or used to! "A woman
shall not wear anything that pertains to a man, nor shall
a man put on a woman's garment; for whoever does
these things is an abomination to the Lord your God"
(Deuteronomy 22:5).

It marks individuality. Not long after the Second World
War a friend of mine was returning by train to London
from the provinces. In the compartment with him was a
little girl who for some years had been evacuated from
the city and had not seen her mother for a long time. The
little one naturally was excited at the prospect of meeting
her mother again on arrival at the station. Teasing her, my
friend said: "But what if she doesn't recognize you? It's
so long since she saw you. Perhaps she's forgotten what
you look like!" The child's bright face clouded at this

suggestion. The idea that her mother would not know her had evidently never occurred to her. It came as a shock, and it took her a minute or two to get over it. Soon, however, she was smiling again as she announced confidently, "It will be all right. Mummy made the dress that I am wearing. If she does not know me by myself, she'll know me by my frock!"

4. Clothing is for adornment.

How dull life would be if people chose their clothes with only warmth in view! We should all be like the Eskimo—at least in winter—and no attention at all would be paid to cloth, color or cut in what we wore. But clothing is for adornment. If you doubt that, go to a popular beach in summer and see what can happen to the human form divine! Perhaps some of us do not need to travel so far to make that discovery!

5. Clothing is for authority.

Clothed with power—even in the sphere of worldly affairs clothing often connotes power. The Queen is clothed with power when she puts on her robes of state. The high court judge is clothed with power when he dons the official garb of his office. The policeman is clothed with power when he wears his uniform.

So it is supremely in the life of the Spirit. Here, too, clothing is power. Elisha was clothed with power when he girt himself with the mantle which had fallen from the shoulders of the ascending Elijah. Aaron, the Hebrew high priest, was clothed with power when he arrayed himself in his sacerdotal garments. Jesus Himself was clothed with power, as the woman, who for twelve years had suffered from a debilitating hemorrhage, realized when the thrill of health flashed through her as she touched the tassel of His robe.

And so Christ told His disciples, "Wait till you are clothed with power."

This gives real authority, not the pompous pretentiousness so frequently associated with earthly rank and position. "I remember a missionary conference," says F. Noel Palmer, "where a senior clergyman annoyed some of his brethren by being rather pompous, and they were talking about it. But a missionary from Africa just said, 'I expect he looks pretty much like the rest of us in his pajamas.'" (*Christ's Way With People*, London, Marshall, Morgan & Scott, 1943, p. 80.)

Such haughtiness—despicable and irritating though it admittedly is—is infinitely preferable to other forms assumed by human pride. A Danish friend of mine told me that nudists from Germany recently have been giving offence to the Danes by appearing naked on the beaches of Denmark. There was quite a furore about it in the Press. The contention, however, was cut short by the common sense comment of one Danish contributor. "I'd rather see twenty naked Germans," he wrote, "than one in uniform!"

One remembers what elephantine fun Thomas Carlyle pokes at pomposity in *Sartor Resartus*. Nevertheless, clothing *does* connote authority.

The Man and the Book

*You search the scriptures . . . yet you
refuse to come to me.* John 5:39, 40

You search the scriptures . . . you will not come to
Me. Scholars tell us that in the original the verb in the
first sentence may be either in the imperative or in the
indicative mood. Either, as in the *King James Version,* the
text may be translated: "Search the scriptures," or as the
Revised Standard Version: "You search the scriptures."
It would seem clear from the context that the latter is the
better rendering. Patently, the verb is in the indicative.
"You search the scriptures." Jesus is not issuing a command
here: He is stating a fact. He is not directing: He is
declaring. He is not urging His hearers to read the Old
Testament: He is owning that they *do* read the Old Testament.

And yet here is the tragedy of it: although diligent
students of the written Word, they were unable to recognize the Living Word, when He stood personally in
their presence. Beyond the sacred page they failed to find
the sacred Person. In fact, the sacred page actually became a paper curtain which concealed Him from them.

Perhaps it will help us to perceive the folly and the
absurdity of their position if we reconstruct the scene in a
modern setting.

Let me ask you to imagine that in 1950 an Australian
aborigine, who has acquired some knowledge of English
and who, hearing that Winston Churchill, then the great-

est living Englishman, is a master of the language, comes to Britain to pursue his studies of the works of the great statesman. He goes into the library of the British Museum in London, asks the librarian for a copy of Churchill's Life and sits down to read it. Soon he is absorbed in the racy narrative, fascinated and enthralled by the author's striding style. Presently, we will suppose, Churchill himself enters the library and, observing that the aborigine is engrossed in a book of his, approaches him and says, "I see that you are interested in my autobiography. May I introduce myself to you personally?" But the aborigine does not even bother to look up. His eyes are glued to the page, and he continues reading, paying no attention whatever to the presence of the author. Only now and then he breaks out, "What a masterly style! What superb literary artistry! What exquisite English!" Churchill observes him in silence. Then the aborigine gets up, goes over to the librarian's desk, and asks if he may see the original manuscript of the book. It is passed to him over the counter. He handles it with reverent care and examines it excitedly. Churchill follows him to the desk and peers over his shoulder. But the aborigine resents this as an impertinent intrusion, returns the precious document to the attendant, and, brushing past the immortal author, hastens out of the building.

"How ridiculous!" you say. Yes! such an attitude would be absurd, but it was the attitude of the Jews to Jesus long ago, and it is the attitude towards Him of many professing Christians today. "You search the scriptures . . . yet you refuse to come to me."

I want to speak to you about the Man and the Book, and there are three things I especially wish to say.

1. The Man was before the Book.

"A world without a Bible! How strange the words sound in our ears! And yet, though few probably realize it, that was the actual condition of this world on which we are now living, so far as it is known, throughout more than one third of its existence as a dwelling place of man. In other words, during the first two thousand five hundred years, that is, until about three thousand five hundred and fifty years ago, there appears to have been no written revelation from God." (Sidney Collett, *The Scriptures of Truth*, London, S. W. Partridge, 1905, p. 1.)

2. The Man is behind the Book.

"I once saw a picture of the Constitution of the United States, very skillfully engraved in copperplate, so that when you looked at it closely it was nothing more than a piece of writing, but when you looked at it from a distance, it was the face of George Washington. The face shone out in the shading of the letters at a little distance, and I saw the person, not the words nor the ideas; and I thought: 'That is the way to look at the Scriptures and understand the thoughts of God; to see in them the face of love shining through and through; not ideas, not doctrines, but Jesus Himself as the Life and Source and sustaining Presence of all our life.'" (A. B. Simpson, *Himself*, London, Marshall, Morgan & Scott, n.d., p. 4.)

A Roman Catholic priest once took one of his parishioners to task for reading the Bible. The parishioner replied: "Your Reverence, I have a search warrant. Jesus said: 'Search the Scriptures!'"

> Break Thou the bread of life,
>   Dear Lord, to me,
> As Thou didst break the loaves
>   Beside the sea;
> Beyond the sacred page
>   I seek Thee, Lord;
> My spirit pants for Thee,
>   O living Word.
>
> Mary Artemisia Lathbury

3. **The Man will be beyond the Book.**

Long after the last Bible has crumbled into dust, the Man will live on. Parchment is not eternal, but the divine Person is. The manuscripts will moulder in decay, but the Man will last forever!

THREE LAWS

Romans 8

Some laws are impossible to keep. In one of the noisiest streets in my native city of Glasgow, there is this notice: "Quiet please: Royal Infirmary." You might as well call for silence at the Niagara Falls!

Some laws are easy to keep. When, for example, I enter a Church of England (which I frequently do) and find myself confronted, either in the *Book of Common Prayer* or on a noticeboard, with "A Table of Kindred and Affinity," and when in that Table I discover that one clause reads: "A man may not marry his grandmother," I am conscious of no serious deprivation or limitation of desire. That law, at any rate, is for me easy to keep.

God's law is both. It is impossible to keep, if we try to conform to it in our own unaided strength, but it is easy to keep when we are filled with the Spirit of God.

A. R. Prentice once pointed to three laws of which mention is made in the eighth chapter of Paul's letter to the Romans, and we may with profit follow the trail of thought he blazed.

1. The law of Moses—dominating.

"God has done what the law, weakened by the flesh, could not do" (Romans 8:3).

"Where there's a law, there's a flaw," they say, but there is no flaw in the law of God.

A father was talking to his small son about the law of gravitation when the boy suddenly asked: "But, Daddy, what happened before they passed that law?"

"The laws of health are as much the laws of God as the Ten Commandments" (*Wayside Pulpit*).

2. The law of sin—subjugating.

"The law of sin and death" (Romans 8:2).

"I see in my members another law at war with the law of my mind and making me captive to the law of sin which dwells in my members" (Romans 7:23).

3. The law of the Spirit of life—emancipating.

"The law of the Spirit of life in Christ Jesus has set me free" (Romans 8:2).

You go to an airport, let us say, to board a plane about to take off on a transatlantic flight. Before you on the runway lies a gigantic machine, weighing hundreds of tons. That machine is subject to a law—the law of gravitation. By itself it cannot rise off the ground. It is absolutely earthbound. Nevertheless you board the plane, believing that it can not only get off its wheels, but wing its way across the wide ocean. It does. Why? Because the law of the spirit called petroleum sets it free from the law of gravitation!

"Man has not learned to fly by defying the law of gravitation but by accepting it and applying the forces of gravity to furthering his purpose." (T. G. Platten, *A Faith for Today*, London, London University Press, 1964, pp. 105–06.)

"He writes the law of God with living fire in our hearts," said Martin Luther, "and consequently the law is not doctrine but life, not word but reality, not a sign but very fulness."

POINT OF NO RETURN

I cannot go back. Judges 11:35 KJV

Some time ago a friend of mine travelled by plane westward across the Atlantic. As the huge machine hurtled through the sky at five hundred miles per hour and at a height of twenty thousand feet, the pilot placed the plane under the automatic controls, left his cabin and came to sit beside my friend. They got into conversation.

"We've just passed the point of no return," the pilot said. "Until we reach that point, if anything goes wrong with the machine, I immediately turn her nose around and head straight back to Britain: once that point has been reached, however, whatever happens, I never go back. I make directly for America." In every human life there are points of no return.

1. There is a point of no return when the child leaves home for the first time.

In his book *Stop the Merry-go-Round,* Don Mallough tells a poignant story. He writes: "During the Klondike Gold Rush of 1898 the quick fortune fever was at a high pitch. Not only men, but even women and couples rushed northward after the yellow gold of the materialists. One adventurous couple even took their ten-year-old son along with them, and exposed him to the rough vulgar crowds in the boom towns of the tundra.

Before a year was out that boy was killed in a needless and senseless accident. With sobered hearts the parents returned to civilization. As they walked down the gang-plank in Seattle old friends called out, 'Did you get any gold?' A heavyhearted father answered, 'Yes, but we lost our son!'"

2. There is a point of no return when the soul loses its innocence.

In his epic *Paradise Lost* Milton pictures the enactment of that tragedy.

> . . . her rash hand in evil hour
> Forth reaching to the Fruit, she pluck'd, she eat:

Earth felt the wound, and Nature from her seat
Sighing through all her Works gave signs of woe,
That all was lost.

3. There is a point of no return where God's mercy ends and His wrath begins.

Not long ago I visited Niagara Falls and saw the sleek, swift-flowing water sliding over the lip of the precipice into the spray-filled abyss below. Not far above the falls I saw the place on the river which is called the Point of No Return. Up to that point it is safe to sail on the broad bosom of the flood, but once venture beyond that point and the rapids rush you over the brink.

4. There is a point of no return when we pass from this world to the next.

In a little churchyard in Lima, N.Y., I saw a tombstone, erected to the memory of a Methodist minister who had labored in those parts and died suddenly in his pulpit. The inscription read: "There is but a beat of the heart, there is but a breath, between this world and the next." Just a single step—but how irreversible the step!

5. There is a point of no return when we decide for Jesus Christ.

You may recall the story of David Brainerd and the Red Indian whom he found hard to persuade to make up his mind to be a Christian. Taking up a pointed stick, Brainerd traced a line in the surface of the soft ground around the hesitating brave. "Decide before you cross that line," he told him.

CHRIST AND THE CROSS

There they crucified him. Luke 23:33

The Bible plays the miser with words. In its use of language it exercises the strictest economy and restraint. Here into one brief sentence it condenses its record of the blackest crime in history. "There they crucified him." That is all it says. There is no attempt at being graphic, dramatic, sensational. There is an utter absence of the detailed realism beloved by the modern imaginative writer. The fact of the crucifixion is stated in a style as stark as the cross itself.

Many artists have striven to depict the scene. Some have shown Christ shrinking from the cross, as the rough soldiers seized His hands and His feet for the purpose of impalement. Others have pictured Him meekly submitting to the ordeal. But there is one artist who delineates the spectacle with singular insight and perceptiveness. He actually pictures Christ struggling to get on to His cross!

His painting hangs in one of the art galleries of Paris. It is a canvas of unforgettable impressiveness, breathtaking in its novel unconventionality. To the right of the painting lies the cross awaiting its victim. On either side is a brutal, burly soldier, each holding a fist full of nails and a heavy hammer, and each glowering malignantly at the central figure. In the middle of the picture stands the Master, a Roman legionary grasping each of His arms as if forcibly restraining Him for some course of action. What is Jesus represented as doing as He wrestles with the soldiers? Is He struggling to get free? Is He trying to get away? No. He is striving to get on to the cross.

It is a striking, even a startling, depictment of what happened at Calvary.

What do we see at the cross?

1. We see what sin does to God.

"Gordon C. Hunter of Toronto tells of a father whose delinquent, teen-age daughter had broken his heart and all but ruined her own life. He had tried everything to correct her, but threats, punishments, pleadings were all of no avail: the girl openly scoffed at his love and refused to acknowledge her guilt. Finally, when the coarseness of her life had reached a new low level, the father called her to him. He rolled up his shirtsleeve, and then took from his pocket a penknife. As the girl watched him, horrified, he plunged the sharp blade into his forearm. 'This is how much I love you,' he told her, 'and this is what you are doing to me.' Deeper and deeper he pushed that blade, and the blood gushed down his arm in a crimson stream until the daughter could stand it no longer. Bursting into tears, she cried: 'Stop it, Dad! Stop it! I never knew! I never knew!'" (Hugh Robert Macdonald, *On Top of the World,* London: Marshall, Morgan & Scott, 1965, p. 46.)

2. We see what sin does to man.

We have all read how, when the famous Italian artist Leonardo da Vinci was about to paint his immortal picture, "The Last Supper," he searched for a young man of pure and radiant countenance to sit as model for his portrait of Christ; and of how, some time later, when nearing the completion of his canvas, he went in quest of someone of such depraved and diabolical aspect that he might sit for the picture of Judas. The artist at last found a man whose face wore so wicked an expression that he felt he might fitly represent the traitor. The man surprised da Vinci by inquiring: "Do you not know me? I am the man who sat for your picture of Christ."

That is what sin does to man.

3. We see what the God-Man did to sin.

From the cross Christ cried, "It is finished." He did not say, "*I* am finished!" He said, "*It* is finished!" What did He mean? Did He mean that His earthly life was finished? That was certainly so. Did He mean that the ceremonial law was finished? That also was true. But there was deeper meaning in His words. A clue as to what that was is provided by a sentence in the Epistle of James. It reads: "Sin, when it is finished, bringeth forth death" (James 1:15, KJV). At Calvary, Christ finished moral evil for all who put their trust in Him. That is what He did to sin.

THE THREE BREADS

The Lord Jesus . . . took bread and when he had given thanks, he broke it, and said, 'This is my body which is for you.' 1 Corinthians 11:23, 24 *We . . . are one bread.* 1 Corinthians 10:17, KJV *How are we to buy bread, so that these people may eat?* John 6:5

Three breads are mentioned in the Bible.

1. There is the bread that we take:

    a. in providence.

        "Give us each day our daily bread" (Luke 11:3).

    b. in regeneration.

        "I am the living bread which came down from heaven; if any one eats of this bread, he will live for ever; and the bread which I shall give for the life of the world is my flesh" (John 6:51).

    c. in Holy Communion.

        "He took bread, and when he had given thanks, he broke it and gave it to them, saying, 'This is my body'" (Luke 22:19, 20).

2. There is the bread that we are.

"We being many are one bread" (1 Corinthians 10:17, KJV).

Look at a loaf. What is it? It is a unity, but behind the unity there is a multiplicity of individual particles, each of which has lost its identity as a grain, to discover, if one may so express it, a larger life within an ampler whole.

So with the church. It is a single entity, yet within it there is an infinitely diversified assortment of individualities. Have you ever been struck, when scanning an average Christian congregation, by the wide variety of human types of which it is composed? And have you ever marvelled as you have reflected that every one of them finds in Christ his personal ideal and discovers within the

Christian community a fuller and a finer life than he could otherwise have known? (Ian Macpherson, *God's Middleman*, London, Epworth Press, 1965, p. 131.)

3. There is the bread that we give.

"If a man is righteous . . . he . . . gives his bread to the hungry" (Ezekiel 18:5, 7).

"Whence shall we buy bread that these may eat?" (John 6:5, KJV).

In one of his travel books, Mr. H. V. Morton tells the beautiful story of the idyll of Sir John Balliol and his wife, the Lady Devorgille. It was Balliol's intention to found a college for poor students at Oxford, and after his death in 1269, his widow completed his design; the foundation bears his name. She did more. When he died, she had his heart embalmed and set in a silver casket which never left her side. It was at the table each time she fed; his place was laid and a meal prepared for many guests. But the food was distributed at the castle gate, day by day, to the poor for whom Balliol had cared. She gave her love to him in the bread she gave to them. (G. Oswald Cornish, *The Unchangeable Friend*, London, Independent Press, 1954, p. 108.)

THE CORN OF HEAVEN

. . . had given them of the corn of heaven.
Psalm 78:24, KJV

Bread! That has been the hungry cry of humanity in every age of its history. Bread! It was the cry of the crowds in ancient Rome in its decadent days. *Panem et circenses.* Bread and games. It was the cry of the famished multitudes of France when in 1789 they hammered on the gates of the Tuileries in Paris. It was the cry of the Russian masses, when in 1917 they stormed the Palace of the Czars.

Notice six things about the manna—what our text beautifully calls the corn of heaven—which God provided for the Israelites in their long march through the desert.

1. It was a mysterious provision.

The very word *manna* is itself a confession of ignorance.

"There was something so strange about it, so mysterious; even about the word *manna*, which literally means, 'What is it?' The children of Israel themselves were fascinated and bewildered by it. And slowly the peculiar word manna has crept into our common religious speech. The word manna has become the symbol of the bread from heaven, that spiritual food without which we are apt to perish by the way." (Geoffrey T. Bellhouse, *Bread from Heaven*, London, Epworth Press, 1963, p. 9.)

2. It was a heavenly provision.

"There is a kind of tree or shrub—a species of tamarisk found in the Middle East—which yields at certain times and in small quantities a kind of gum, to which the name of manna has been given, in the belief that it really was, or that it resembled, the manna by which the Israelites were fed." (Kitto's *Dictionary of the Bible.*)

3. It was a homely provision.

Manna was not luxury, it was necessity. It was not

cake, it was bread. It was not a condiment or a confection, but substantial food.

4. It was a daily provision.

"The pupils of Rabbi Simon ben Jochai once asked him, 'Why did not Jehovah give to Israel enough manna to suffice them for a whole year at one time instead of meting it out daily?' The rabbi replied, 'I will answer you with a parable. There was once a king who had a son to whom he gave a certain sum once a year. It so happened that the day on which this allowance was due was the only day in the year when the father saw his son. So he changed his plan and gave his son each day his allowance for that day only, and then the son visited his father every morning. So was it with Israel. Each father, being dependent on the manna sent by Jehovah each day for the support of his family, had his mind devoted thereby to the great Giver.'" (Edward Clodd, *A Sketch of Jewish History*, London, Kegan, Paul and French, 1889, p. 157.)

Our Lord taught us to pray: "Give us each day our daily bread" (Luke 11:3).

5. It was an adequate provision.

A Spartan old doctor was accustomed to say, "One meal a day is enough for a lion, and it ought to suffice for a man." We are not told how many meals the Israelites made of the daily supply of manna, but we do know that the divine provision was sufficient until they reached the Promised Land. There was no need for manna in a land flowing with milk and honey. So "the manna ceased on the morrow, when they ate of the produce of the land; and the people of Israel had manna no more, but ate of the fruit of the land of Cānaan that year" (Joshua 5: 12).

6. It was a provision which had to be appropriated personally.

A man might starve in a bakery capable of supplying the needs of a whole city, if he did not put out his hand and partake of the bread.

God's Acceptance of Us

God is not ashamed to be called their God. Hebrews 11:16

In his fine book *The Face of Christ,* W. W. Weeks tells a touching story which may well form a frontispiece to our study of the God who is not ashamed. He writes: "Some years ago there appeared in Scotland a very brilliant young preacher. Wherever he went, thousands flocked to hear him, and no church was found large enough to accommodate the throng. One day he was to preach in St. George's West, Edinburgh. Hours before the service was to begin, thousands thronged the street outside, and when the hour arrived for the doors to open there was a great rush to gain admittance. On the very crest of that human wave was a very little old woman, wearing a faded shawl and an old-fashioned bonnet, but on her face was registered an eager expectation. As she entered the church she asked an usher to seat her near the front as her hearing was not good. He thrust her into the first pew inside the door, telling her she must be content with any place that day. Soon the great church was packed and the time for the service arrived. The old pastor entered, followed by the brilliant young orator. During the preliminaries, the young man was seen carefully scanning the congregation. Suddenly, he rose, left the pulpit by a rear door, and soon appeared in the aisle. Walking down to the door, he threw his arm round the old lady in the faded shawl and reverently kissed her. Then, taking her on his arm, he led her up the aisle and one of Scotland's peers was proud to give his seat to the preacher's mother!"

He was not ashamed to call her *Mother*, nor is God ashamed to call us His sons and daughters.

1. He has reason to be ashamed of us.

Every one of us, in one way or another, has brought discredit and disgrace upon His holy name. He might have disowned us and cast us off, repudiating any association with us, but, blessed be His name, He hasn't. He is not ashamed to be called our God.

2. Are we ever ashamed of Him?

The question seems ridiculous, yet Jesus Himself envisaged that very possibility. "Whoever is ashamed of me," He said, ". . . in this adulterous and sinful generation, of him will the Son of man also be ashamed, when he comes in the glory of his Father with the holy angels" (Mark 8:38).

Many years ago I heard a moving story about a widowed mother who had stinted herself to the point of starvation that she might give her only son a medical education. In due course he became a brilliant surgeon, mixing with the elite of the land on equal terms. He seldom saw his mother. Though he would not have admitted it even to himself, he was secretly ashamed of her. She, for her part, never ceased to love him. She never ventured to cross the threshold of his magnificent city mansion, but every now and then she surreptitiously crept up to it in the hope of catching sight of him. One day, on her way home, after doing this, she was struck down in the street just outside her son's house by a heavy vehicle, and was picked up unconscious and on the point of death. The most obvious thing was to take her to the nearest doctor's residence. Imagine the son's feelings as he looked into the face of the dying form on the couch in his surgery—the face of the mother of whom he had been ashamed!

3. **Wonder of wonders, He is not ashamed of us.**

> Then will He own my worthless name
> Before His Father's face,
> And in the new Jerusalem
> Appoint my soul a place.

> Isaac Watts

STICK TO IT!

The Spirit said to Philip, "Go up and join this chariot." Acts 8:29

The word translated *join* in the text is a pictorial one. It means literally: glue yourself to the chariot; stick to it like grim death; hang on tenaciously until your mission is accomplished.

There are things in life to which we should all do well to adhere like that.

1. Stick to proven truth.

When something has been divinely revealed to you in such a way that, when the revelation first came, you were absolutely sure of it, do not lightly set such revelation aside nor question its validity because of a change in your condition or circumstances.

2. Stick to tried friends.

Remember your Shakespeare.

> The friends thou hast, and their adoption tried,
> Grapple them to thy soul with hoops of steel;
> But do not dull thy palm with entertainment
> Of each new-hatched, unfledged comrade.
>
> Hamlet 1:3

3. Stick to your unfinished tasks.

"I never knew a man good for anything in this world," wrote John Stuart Blackie, "who, when he had a job to do, did not know how to stick at it until it was done."

4. Stick to the house of God.

Do you know the *A B C* of church membership?

a. Attend the church.

"Not neglecting to meet together, as is the habit of some" (Hebrews 10:25).

b. Befriend the church.

"As we have opportunity, let us do good

to all men, and especially to those who are of the household of faith" (Galatians 6:10).

c. Commend the church.

"In everything . . . adorn the doctrine of God our Saviour" (Titus 2:10).

"Let your light so shine before men, that they may see your good works and give glory to your Father who is in heaven" (Matthew 5:16).

JUDAS AND JESUS

He [Judas] went and hanged himself. Matthew 27:5
Jesus whom you killed by hanging him on a tree. Acts 5:30

Judas hanged! Jesus hanged! What grim irony—the same fate seemingly befalling the best and the worst of men! On the first Good Friday, two gallows raised their gaunt forms in the vicinity of Golgotha. One bore the world's blackest criminal: the other bore the One who ever wore the white flower of a blameless life. Apparently, the universe is indifferent to moral distinctions. Good and evil alike meet the same dark doom.

Is that so? No, it is not so. Although superficially similar, those two trees, with their blood-red fruit, were as different as one that bears poisoned berries from one that bears rich, luscious fruit.

1. **The hanging of Judas was suicide, the hanging of Jesus was sacrifice.**

2. **The hanging of Judas was expressive of remorse, the hanging of Jesus brought redemption.**

The Jews have an awful epithet which they sometimes apply to Christ. They call Him *the Hanged.* That is meant to denigrate and depreciate Him, but it is His crowning glory.

3. **The hanging of Judas was the symbol of a soul's despair; the hanging of Jesus is the emblem of a whole world's hope.**

Let us hang on Him who on the cross was hanged for us.

THE THREE CUPS OF CHRIST

They offered him wine to drink, mingled with gall; but when he tasted it, he would not drink it. Matthew 27:34 *Shall I not drink the cup which the Father has given me?* John 18:11 *And he took a cup, and when he had given thanks he said, "Take this, and divide it among yourselves."* Luke 22:17

There are three cups of Christ in the New Testament. A cup can be a symbol of supply or a trophy of success, an emblem of sorrow or a figure of joy. It was all these to Christ.

1. There was the cup He declined.

"When he tasted it, he would not drink."

The giving of this cup was a ministry of mercy. It was a drug designed to mitigate His pain. He refused it because He wanted to die with clear brain and full consciousness of all that was happening to Him. Had He taken that drug, He could not have *tasted* death for every man (Hebrews 2:9).

2. There was the cup He drained.

"Shall I not drink?"

There is a grand story of Alexander the Great's confidence in his friend and physician. When the physician had mixed him a potion for his sickness, a letter was put into Alexander's hand, warning him not to drink the mixture because it was poisoned. He held the letter in the one hand and the cup in the other, and, in the presence of his friend and physician, drank up the draught. After he had drained the cup, he made his friend look at that letter and judge of his confidence in him. Alexander had unstaggering faith in his friend, which did not admit of doubt. "See now," he said, "how I have trusted you." Charles Haddon Spurgeon. (Quoted in *Bible Sermon Outlines*, Ed. by Ian Macpherson, Abingdon Press, Nashville & New York, 1966, pp. 115–16.)

One can transform the contents of a cup if one can change the hand from which one takes it. (W. E. Sangster, *The Pure in Heart,* London, Epworth Press, 1954, p. 151.)

3. There was the cup He dispensed.

"Take this, and divide it among yourselves."

You may recall the famous story of how once at a Communion service in Edinburgh, where Dr. John Duncan was officiating, there was a poor woman who, crouched weeping in her pew, declined the cup which was handed to her by the distributing elder. Dr. Duncan saw this and was touched to the depths of his being. Coming down from his place at the Holy Table, he seized the cup from the hand of the elder and thrust it into that of the woman, crying, "Take it, woman, take it: it's for sinners!"

It *is*—for *repentant* sinners!

The Relevance of God

I am the Lord, . . . therefore. . . . Malachi 3:6 KJV

The London *Daily Telegraph* of October 31, 1967 reported a weekend conference of Christians and Communists which had just been held in Bevindon New Town, England. Presiding was Bishop Spacely-Trellis, who declared that the conference had been a resounding success. Asked if there was much common ground between the Christians and the Communists, he replied, "We found that we agreed about almost everything—housing, education, the social services, Vietnam—everything that matters in the world today." "Was the subject of God raised at all?" the reporter ventured to inquire. At this the Bishop is said to have looked pained. "My dear chap," he said, "at a meeting like this one must stick to essentials."

Is God relevant? Is He in our sophisticated, scientific age to be reckoned among the "essentials"?

We think He is, and we can adduce three cogent reasons in support of our contention. God is relevant to our time:

1. **Because of the sense of mystery and the search for meaning.**

2. **Because of the feeling of failure and the quest for success.**

3. **Because of the consciousness of loneliness and the longing for fellowship.**

WHERE THE CHRISTIAN IS TO TRAIN HIS SIGHTS

1 John 3:20,21; Hebrews 12:1,2; Hebrews 12:3-9; 2 Peter 3:10-14; Philippians 3:14; Titus 2:11-13; 2 Peter 1:9; 2 Corinthians 4:17-18

1. Not in, but out.

"Whenever our hearts condemn us; for God is greater than our hearts, and he knows everything. Beloved, if our hearts do not condemn us, we have confidence before God" (1 John 3:20,21).

2. Not on, but off.

"Therefore, since we are surrounded by so great a cloud of witnesses, let us also lay aside every weight, and sin which clings so closely, and let us run with perseverance the race that is set before us, looking to Jesus the pioneer and perfecter of our faith" (Hebrews 12:1,2).

3. Not down, but up.

"[Jesus] is seated at the right hand of the throne of God. Consider him" (Hebrews 12:2,3).

4. Not around, but forward.

"But the day of the Lord will come like a thief" (2 Peter 3:10).

5. Not backward, but onward.

"One thing I do, forgetting what lies behind and straining forward to what lies ahead, I press on toward the goal for the prize of the upward call of God in Christ Jesus" (Philippians 3:13,14).

6. Not near, but far.

"Whoever lacks these things is blind and shortsighted and has forgotten that he was cleansed from his old sins" (2 Peter 1:9).

7. Not at time, but at eternity.

"This slight momentary affliction is preparing for us an eternal weight of glory beyond all comparison, because we look not to the things that are seen but to the things that are unseen; for the things that are seen are transient, but the things that are unseen are eternal" (2 Corinthians 4:17,18).

(Henry W. Frost, *Outline Bible Studies*, London: Marshall, Morgan & Scott, 1924, p. 300.)

Calling to him a child, [Jesus] put him in the midst of [the disciples,] and said: "Truly, I say to you, unless you turn and become like children, you will never enter the kingdom of heaven. Whoever humbles himself like this child, he is the greatest in the kingdom of heaven. Matthew 18:2-4

How different Jesus is from everybody else! This is seen even in the little things he did while on earth. Any other teacher would have taken that small boy and set him in the midst of the disciples and told him, "Be a good boy. Study hard. Do what your parents tell you, and some day you will be a big man like Peter, James or John." But Jesus completely reverses that. He puts the little lad in the midst of the big men and bids them become like him! Who but Jesus would have done that? And yet what piercing insight it reveals into the nature of moral reality.

What are the lessons that a little child can teach us?

1. **You do not have to be big in order to be loved.**

2. **You do not have to pay in order to be welcome.**

3. **You do not have to be active in order to be attractive.**

4. **You do not have to be great in order to be influential.**

5. **You do not have to be an orator to make your wants known.**

Recall your Tennyson:

> But what am I?
>> An infant crying in the night.
>> An infant crying for the light.
>> And with no language but a cry.

What language is more eloquent in a mother's ears than that?

PAUL'S THREE CHARGES TO TIMOTHY
AN INDUCTION SERMON

1 Timothy 1:18,19; 6:13,14; 2 Timothy 4:1,2; 1 Timothy 5:21

Paul uses great plainness of speech in addressing Timothy. He does not mince his words or veil his meaning. He talks urgently in the manner of one who means business because time is rapidly running out.

There are three charges which he solemnly lays upon the soul of his junior colleague.

It will be for our spiritual profit to study them for a little together on this important occasion.

1. There is a personal charge.

"This charge I commit to you, Timothy, my son, in accordance with the prophetic utterances which pointed to you, that inspired by them you may wage the good warfare, holding faith and a good conscience" (1 Timothy 1:18,19).

"In the presence of God who gives life to all things,

and of Christ Jesus who in his testimony before Pontius Pilate made the good confession, I charge you to keep the commandment unstained and free from reproach until the appearing of our Lord Jesus Christ" (1 Timothy 6:13,14).

2. There is a homiletical charge.

"I charge you in the presence of God and of Christ Jesus who is to judge the living and the dead, and by his appearing and his kingdom: preach the word, be urgent in season and out of season, convince, rebuke and exhort, be unfailing in patience and in teaching" (2 Timothy 4:1,2).

3. There is a pastoral charge.

"In the presence of God and of Christ Jesus and of the elect angels I charge you to keep these rules without favor, doing nothing from partiality" (1 Timothy 5:21).

SERMONS IN STONES

What do these stones mean to you? Joshua 4:6

In Shakespeare's *As You Like It*, the exiled duke speaks of finding sermons in stones. Not everybody can do that. To most people stones are just awkward solid obstacles which beset one's path: to some perceptive souls, they glitter with mystic meanings.

It is this power to perceive which marks the difference between one person and another. Of this, the history of our discoveries and inventions provides conclusive proof. As one has said, "Almost all the great discoveries have been made by observing trifles. Children playing with spectacles, or the swinging of a lamp, are incidents small enough, but the telescope and the pendulum were thus given to men. Watt watched the uplifting of the kettle lid, and thus learned the force of the steam giant. Edison, looking at the smoke on his lamp chimney, thereby was able to give us the electric lamp."

Can you see as they saw? Perhaps not. Like me, you may lack the creative imagination and the specialized knowledge they possessed. But you can see far more in things than you normally see if only you will contemplate them reflectively.

Pick up a stone. What sermons do you see in it?

1. There is in it a sermon on unity.

Few unities are more cohesive than that of stone. It is comprised of thousands of microscopic particles, but, as you look at the stone, you are not aware of this. It seems one object, and indeed it is. There is in it a sermon on unity.

2. There is in it a sermon on durability.

"Back among the beautiful White Mountains of New Hampshire is a most unusual rock formation which has been known for years as 'The Old Man of the Mountain.' It stands out against the sky, a perfect profile of a man's head, with a resemblance to the figure of an old pioneer with his coonskin cap that is almost uncanny. Years ago Nathaniel Hawthorne immortalized it in his story, *The Great Stone Face*, which is the tale of a boy who became great through keeping a great ideal before himself. Looking up at the face on the mountainside, the boy invested it with personality and strove, year after year, to imitate the virtues he believed his hero of the mountain to possess. Just as Ernest, in Hawthorne's story, reached the heights by keeping his eyes on the great stone face, so we may yet redeem life by lifting up our eyes to the hills." (Roy L. Smith, *Suburban Christians,* New York, Harpers Brothers, 1933, pp. 29, 30.)

3. **There is in it a sermon of warning on the tragic possibility of becoming spiritually dead and cold as a stone.**

When the body of David Livingstone was deposited in the vault in the nave of Westminster Abbey where it now rests, Mr. Punch, England's journalistic jester, laid aside for once his bauble and bells and assumed a serious tone as he said, "Let marble crumble, this is *Livingstone.*"

"Like living stones be yourselves built into a spiritual house" (1 Peter 2:5).

Handling Your Talent

Matthew 25:14-30

Are you *talented?* The term has been imported into colloquial speech from Christ's parable of the talents. From this parable we learn that it is possible to do any one of three things with one's talent.

1. **It can be bartered.**
"He who had received the five talents went at once

and traded with them; and he made five talents more"
(v.16).

2. It can be banked.
"You ought to have invested my money with the
bankers, and at my coming I should have received what
was my own with interest" (v.27).

3. It can be buried.
"He who had received the one talent went and dug
in the ground and hid his master's money" (v.18).

THE WORLD ON THE CROSS

The world has been crucified to me. Galatians 6:14

Here Paul uses a terrific figure. He pictures the world
on a cross. We are familiar with the concept of Christ
on the cross and of the Christian on the cross, but the
idea of the world on a cross is one of startling novelty
and gripping power.

On what cross is the world impaled?

1. William Jennings Bryan spoke of the world being crucified on a cross of gold.
"You shall not press down upon the brow of labor this
crown of thorns. You shall not crucify mankind upon a
cross of gold." Speech at the National Democratic Con-
vention, Chicago, 1896.

2. William Edwin Sangster spoke of the world as crucified upon a clock.

"All our life we have been the slaves of time. If it were not prostituting the most solemn metaphor we know, we might speak of half mankind as crucified upon a clock." (*Westminster Sermons,* London, Epworth Press, 1961, Vol. 2, p. 18.)

3. Paul spoke of the world being crucified on Christ's cross.

On the cross he did not see the waxen figure of catholic piety: he saw the world, with all its glitter and glamor, hanging dead, utterly helpless to allure or seduce him.

THE GATES OF HOLY SCRIPTURE

Lift up your heads, O gates! Psalm 24:7

There are many wonderful gates in the world. Recollecting at random, I remember the gates of Holyrood Palace in Edinburgh, those of the Tuileries in Paris, and those of the cathedral at San Francisco.

The Bible, too, has many gates. Let us think of four of them.

1. The narrow gate of salvation.

"The gate is narrow and the way is hard, that leads to life, and those who find it are few" (Matthew 7:14).

2. The beautiful gate of restoration.

"A man lame from birth was being carried, whom they laid daily at the gate of the temple which is called Beautiful to ask alms of those who entered the temple. Seeing Peter and John about to go into the temple, he asked for alms. And Peter directed his gaze at him, with John, and said, 'Look at us.' And he fixed his attention upon them, expecting to receive something from them. But Peter said, 'I have no silver and gold, but I give you what I have; in the name of Jesus Christ of Nazareth, walk.' And he took him by the right hand and raised him up; and immediately his feet and ankles were made strong. And leaping up he stood and walked and entered the temple with them, walking and leaping and praising God" (Acts 3:2-8).

As the witty old preacher put it, "He asked for *alms* and he got *legs.*"

3. **The iron gate of frustration.**

"They came to the iron gate leading into the city" (Acts 12:10).

4. **The glorious gate of eternal habitation.**

"And the twelve gates were twelve pearls, each of the gates made of a single pearl" (Revelation 21:21).

There come to mind in this connection the spacious lines of William Walsham How:

From earth's wide bounds, from ocean's farthest coast,
Through gates of pearl streams in the countless host,
Singing to Father, Son, and Holy Ghost:
Alleluia! Alleluia!

Is Your Education Complete?

We know that you are a teacher. John 3:2

There is a lovely story of an old local preacher, a shepherd from the hills, who was once invited to a dinner given by the members of a scientific society in a small town in the north of England. He was asked to make a speech and, although keenly conscious of his intellectual and educational limitations in such a brilliant company, he felt it was too good a chance to miss of witnessing for his Master. Rising slowly to his feet, he began, "Gentlemen, I am not versed in all your arts and sciences, but, as you see, a plain and simple man. I don't know much about astronomy, but I *do* know 'The Bright and Morning Star.' I don't know much about botany, but I *do* know 'The Lily of the Valley' and 'The Rose of Sharon.' I don't know much about geography, but I *do* know my way to the Cross of Calvary."

Is *your* education complete?

1. In botany?

Not until you know "the true vine" (John 15:1).

2. In geology?

Not unless you are acquainted with "The Rock" (Deuteronomy 32:4).

3. In chemistry?

Not unless you are familiar with the great catalytic. "But by the same word the heavens and earth that now exist have been stored up for fire, being kept until the day of judgment and destruction of ungodly men" (2 Peter 3:7).

4. In mathematics?

Not until you have calculated the dimensions of the love of Christ. "I bow my knees before the Father, . . . that . . . He may grant you . . . power to comprehend with all the saints what is the breadth and length and height and depth, and to know the love of Christ which surpasses knowledge, that you may be filled with all the fulness of God" (Ephesians 3:14,18,19).

5. In biology?

Not unless you know Him whom to know is life eternal. "This is eternal life, that they know thee the only true God, and Jesus Christ whom thou hast sent" (John 17:3).

6. In geography?

Not unless you know your way to Bethlehem, the Mount of the Sermon, Calvary, Olivet and the Upper Room.

7. In astronomy?

Not unless you know "the bright morning star" (Revelation 22:16).

GOD'S BEST GIFT

If you then, who are evil, know how to give good gifts to your children, how much more will the heavenly Father give the Holy Spirit to those who ask Him! Luke 11:13

It would be interesting to discover precisely *why* the disciples asked Jesus to teach them to pray. Several things might have prompted them to make the request. Perhaps it was the beauty of the words Jesus used in framing His petitions. Or perhaps it was the wonderful way in which His prayers worked and were answered. Or, again, perhaps it was because of the ecstasy which He experienced in communion with His Father. We do not know. All we do know is that there was something about His intercessions which induced His followers to beg Him to instruct them in the holy art of prayer.

Have we, I wonder, a clue in what is recorded to have happened not long before? "In that same hour [Jesus] rejoiced in the Holy Spirit and said, 'I thank Thee, Father'" (Luke 10:21).

Was it this praying in the Spirit which introduced the disciples to a new dimension of devotion? Never before had they heard anything like it. It cut new ground for them in the country of prayer, startled them as those were startled who listened for the first time to human voices on gramophone, telephone and radio.

This, they instinctively felt, was the best gift of all. This was supremely what to pray for.

1. It is the Father who longs to give the gift.

"I remember one dark November night in the slums of Edinburgh coming across a man lying on the pavement in a state of hopeless intoxication. When I tried to help him to his feet he put up a stout resistance. I discovered on investigation that the wretched creature was desperately clutching a doll that he was carrying home to his sick little daughter." (Robert Menzies, *The Magnet of the Heart*, London, James Clarke, n.d., p. 66.)

Even a debauched and dissolute father had a gift for his child. How much more our holy Father in heaven!

2. It is the Holy Spirit who is the gift.

Who or what is the Holy Spirit? Some apply to Him the nasty neuter. They speak of *it* where they should say *He,* for the Holy Spirit is a person. He is not just the activity of God, an emanation from God, or an aspect of God. He is God, Third of the Holy Three. So when we receive Him as a gift we receive a person, as on the lower level of ordinary life a bridegroom receives his bride as a gift from her parents, or as adopting parents receive a baby from his or her natural parents.

3. It is only children who can receive this gift.

The divine donation is reserved for those who belong to the family. Of the Holy Spirit our Lord expressly says, ". . . the world cannot receive . . . Him" (John 14:17). The boon is solely for the believer. The blessing is for the sons and daughters of the household of faith.

4. It is simply by asking that the gift is to be got.

Even the human spirit is a gift from God. "The spirit returns to God who gave it" (Ecclesiastes 12:7). So is the Holy Spirit a gift. Now, you cannot earn a gift; you cannot buy it; you cannot merit it. All you can do is to take it with beggar's hands.

THE BODY OF CHRIST

You are the body of Christ. 1 Corinthians 12:27

It is important to notice precisely what Paul says here. Perhaps the best way of pinpointing that will be to observe, first, what he does *not* say.

He does not say, "You are the *Spirit* of Christ." Elsewhere, the apostle argues that all believers *have* the Spirit of Christ. "Anyone who does not have the Spirit of Christ does not belong to him" (Romans 8:9). Nor does Paul say, "You are the *mind* of Christ." In another place he does affirm that the Church *has* the mind of Christ. "We have the mind of Christ" (1 Corinthians 2:16). But he does not claim that the Chuch *is* the mind of Christ.

Now note what he does say. Having cleared the ground by surveying these, we are ready to turn to the positive. "You are the body of Christ."

What body? Patently, not the body that grew in Mary's womb and groaned upon the cross; not the body that lay in the tomb and strode from its darkness into the glory of the first Easter dawn. Not that physical body! It is now in heaven—the glorified humanity of Jesus.

The body here referred to is the mystical body of Christ: the community of the converted, the society of the saved, the household of the holy. The figure is infinitely suggestive.

1. **The body is a means of identification.**

2. **The body is a system of organization.**

3. **The body is a medium of communication.**

4. **The body is a vehicle of inspiration.**

5. **The body is the instrument of procreation.**

6. **The body is the organ of operation.**

Spiritual Suntan

We all, with unveiled face, beholding the glory of the Lord, are being changed into his likeness from one degree of glory to another; for this comes from the Lord who is the Spirit. 2 Corinthians 3:18

You must have noticed, as I have, that when people come to the coast for their summer vacations, they usually arrive pale and pasty of face. After a few days' exposure to the sun, however, their countenances take on new complexions. Something of the sunlight communicates itself to them, and they become bronzed and healthy looking. They get suntanned.

Of course, there are artificial ways of getting brown. You can go into a pharmacy and buy a bottle of chocolate-colored fluid which you can apply to your face to make you look as if you had just had a month's holiday in the Bahamas!

Most people prefer the real thing. For them, there is no substitute for the sun, and only by exposure to its tincturing rays do they wish to have their appearance transformed.

To this there is a spiritual parallel. The Bible speaks of God as a sun (Psalm 84:11), and by basking in the warm glow of His holiness and love one acquires a spiritual suntan which betokens health of soul.

Reference is made in the Book of God to three persons whose faces shone in this way.

1. There was Moses.

"When Moses came down from Mount Sinai, with the two tables of the testimony in his hand as he came down from the mountain, Moses did not know that the skin of his face shone because he had been talking with God. And when Aaron and all the people of Israel saw Moses, behold, the skin of his face shone, and they were afraid to come near him" (Exodus 34:29,30).

Thus spiritual suntan symbolized the glory of a kept law.

2. There was Jesus.

"And after six days Jesus took with Him Peter and James and John his brother, and led them up a high mountain apart. And he was transfigured before them, and his face shone like the sun, and his garments became white as light" (Matthew 17:1,2).

This spiritual suntan symbolizes the glory of the practice of the Presence.

"Holiness," someone has said, "is not a snapshot: it is a time exposure."

3. There was Stephen.

"Gazing at him, all who sat in the council saw that his face was like the face of an angel" (Acts 6:15).

This spiritual suntan symbolized the splendor of a Spirit-filled life. Of Stephen, we are told that he was "full of the Holy Spirit" (Acts 7:55).

*After six days Jesus took with Him Peter and James
and John his brother, and led them up a high mountain
apart. . . . Lo, a bright cloud overshadowed them. . . .
They were coming down the mountain.* Matthew 17:1,5,9

Take the three parts of this thrilling story of the Trans-
figuration of Christ—the ascent, the cloud on the summit,
and the descent—as a parable of human experience. They
represent three periods of our common life.

1. **The climbing.**
Youth is ever on the climb.

2. **The summit.**
Hermon is seldom without a cloud. Summer and winter,
across its snow-capped top, there is almost always a passing cloud. So it is with life. A cloud will come, however
high we climb.

3. **The descent.**
We are not so sure of ourselves coming down.

Robert Burns employs the same poignant figure to
describe life in his poem "John Anderson, my jo."

> John Anderson my jo, John
> We clamb the hill thegither;
> And monie a canty day, John,
> We've had wi' ane anither.
> Now we maun totter down, John,
> And hand in hand we'll go,

And sleep thegither at the foot,
John Anderson my jo.

What the Love of God Is Like

Psalm 103:13; Isaiah 66:13; Isaiah 62:5

1. It is like a father's pity.

"As a father pities his children, so the Lord pities those who fear Him" (Psalm 103:13).

2. It is like a mother's comfort.

"As one whom his mother comforts, so I will comfort you" (Isaiah 66:13).

We do well in this regard to remind ourselves of the wise words of J. H. Jowett: "God comforts us, not that we may be *comfortable,* but that we may be *comforters.*"

3. It is like a bridegroom's delight.

"As the bridegroom rejoices over the bride, so shall your God rejoice over you" (Isaiah 62:5).

The Four Calls of the Mother Bird

O Jerusalem, Jerusalem, killing the prophets and stoning those who are sent to you! How often would I have gathered your children together as a hen gathers her brood under her wings, and you would not! Matthew 23:37

John Bunyan in his *Pilgrim's Progress* carefully notes that there are four calls that a mother bird uses in summoning her brood.

1. **The call of night**—when the summons is to rest.

2. **The call to eat**—when the summons is to nourishment.

3. **The call of danger**—when the summons is to protection.

4. **The call of love**—when the summons is to experience her warm affection. Christ summons us in all these ways.

CALL THE WITNESSES!

You shall be my witnesses. Acts 1:8

A famous British lawyer of a former day, Reader Harris, once made the arresting remark: "When I have a poor case in the courts, I prepare an eloquent speech: when I have a good case, I simply call the witnesses."

Christianity is on trial for its life today, but there is a good case for it: so call the witnesses! What is there about a witness which makes his testimony so impressive?

1. A witness was there when it happened.

His evidence is more powerful and coercive than the most brilliant and persuasive speech from a barrister who did not witness the occurrence. Being there, and seeing for yourself, are the chief qualifications of a witness.

2. A witness is bound to tell the total truth.

If he holds anything back, he is committing perjury, a very serious crime.

3. A witness is out for a verdict.

Knowing the facts, as he does, he cannot help being emotionally involved in the trial, and passionately concerned to influence the jury accordingly in making their fateful decision.

What To Do With Your Enemies

Love your enemies. Matthew 5:44

No man is without enemies. If anybody is, he is not a man, or maybe he has lived too lax or too long. On being told of the passing of someone of whom it was said that he died leaving no enemy, Joseph Parker is reported to have remarked, "He should have died long ago."

The Bible has much to say about enemies. In our sophisticated age we are not so likely to know who our enemies are; but in biblical times, people were in no doubt.

They knew who their enemies were all right, and they were faced with the problem of what to do with them.

We have foes too. How are we to treat them? There are three possibilities.

1. We can injure them.
That will put us *below* our enemies.

2. We can have our revenge.
That will put us *on a par* with our enemies.

3. We can forgive and favor them.
That will put us *above* our enemies.

*When he comes, he will convince the world of sin . . .
because they do not believe in me.* John 16:8,9

Many years ago, on becoming a Christian, I secretly registered the resolve, "I will endeavor so to live, that if people do not like me, it will be a reflection on them and not on me."

How far I have managed to keep that vow I do not know. But I do know this: Jesus Christ succeeded perfectly in living like that!

His character and His career were such that they put His critics in the wrong. By their refusal to accept His claims they thought that they were casting an aspersion upon Him, but the irony of it was, that by so doing, they were casting an ineradicable aspersion on themselves. They were guilty of the sin of not believing.

One recalls in this connection the oft-told story of the boorish visitor to the art gallery, who, after a brisk walk through salons where immortal masterpieces hung, remarked contemptuously to one of the attendants, "I don't think much of your pictures!" To which the attendant quietly replied, "The pictures are not on trial: the visitors are!" Such Philistinism is recorded even of so robust a thinker as Thomas Carlyle, but the supreme example of it is that of Christ's contemporary critics.

They were guilty of the sin of not believing. Are we?

1. Do we believe in Christ as the Lord of all good life?

74

2. **Do we believe in Christ as the Saviour of the human soul?**

3. **Do we believe in Christ as the Harmonist of history?**

WHAT CHRIST SHED FOR US

John 11:35;   Matthew 26:28, KJV;   Acts 2:33

There are differences between people just as there are differences between trees. Some trees—we call them evergreens—never shed their leaves. Others are deciduous, and their foliage falls with the passing of the summer. Human beings are the same. Some shed nothing; nothing, that is, which is of any value to them. They are not morally deciduous. They will never divest themselves of their affected dignity. They never give liberally to any deserving cause. They have, as we say, nothing to give away. Others are ready to shed even their blood.

Think of what Christ shed for us.

1. **He shed tears.**

The shortest verse in the Bible contains its greatest truth. "Jesus wept" (John 11:35).

2. **He shed blood.**

"This is my blood . . . which is shed for many" (Matthew 26:28 KJV).

3. **He shed the Spirit.**

"[Christ] hath shed forth this, which ye now see and hear" (Acts 2:33 KJV).

75

Revelation; 1:5,6; 4:8; 14:3; 5:11-13.

The Book of Revelation, for all its blood and thunder, is essentially a book of song. It is highly significant that the Bible should close with bursts of music. Music has been memorably defined as discord resolving itself into harmony. By its very nature, music cannot properly end in discord. So, says the Apocalypse, despite all the clashing discordancies of the ages, there is going to be concord at last. History is to end in harmony.

In the Book of Revelation reference is made to four songs.

1. **There is a solo.**

"To Him who loves us and has freed us from our sins by his blood and made us a kingdom, priests to his God and Father, to him be glory and dominion for ever and ever. Amen" (Revelation 1:5,6).

2. **There is a quartet.**

"The four living creatures, each of them with six wings, are full of eyes all round and within, and day and night they never cease to sing, "Holy, holy, holy, is the Lord God Almighty, who was and is and is to come" (Revelation 4:8).

3. **There is an item by the choir.**

"They sing a new song before the throne and before the

76

four living creatures and before the elders. No one could learn that song except the hundred and forty-four thousand who had been redeemed from the earth" (Revelation 14:3).

4. **There is tumultuous singing by the whole congregation.**

"Then I looked, and I heard around the throne and the living creatures and the elders the voice of many angels, numbering myriads of myriads and thousands of thousands, saying with a loud voice, 'Worthy is the Lamb who was slain, to receive power and wealth and wisdom and might and honor and glory and blessing!' And I heard every creature in heaven and on earth and in the sea, and all therein, saying: 'To him who sits upon the throne and to the Lamb be blessing and honor and glory and might for ever and ever!' " (Revelation 5:11-3).

THE COMMUNION OF THE SPIRIT

The communion of the Holy Ghost, be with you all. 2 Corinthians 13:14, KJV

This familiar benediction, which invokes upon us the "communion of the Holy Ghost," has probably a deeper meaning in it than has generally been recognized. The word *communion*—Greek, *koinonia*—signifies the having in common. It is used of the fellowship of believers one with another, and also of their mutual fellowship with God. The Holy Spirit dwelling in us is the agent through whom the community of life and love is effected and maintained.

Consider the Spirit in His various offices of communication.

1. As the Spirit of Life, He is our regeneration.

The new birth is not a change of nature as it is sometimes defined: it is rather the communication of the divine nature, and the Holy Spirit is now the mediator through whom this life is transmitted.

2. As the Spirit of holiness, He is our sanctification.

Self is not powerful enough to conquer self, nor the human spirit to get the victory over the human flesh. That is like a drowning man with his right hand laying hold on his left hand, only that both may sink beneath the waves.

3. As the Spirit of glory, He is and will be our transfiguration.

"The spirit of glory and of God rests upon you" (1 Peter 4:14). It seems to us that the sanctification taking place at the manifestation of our incarnate Lord, will be as the instantaneous photograph compared with the Spirit's slow and patient limning of the image of Christ in our present state. "We shall all be changed, in a moment, in the twinkling of an eye" (1 Corinthians 15:51,52).

(A. J. Gordon, *The Ministry of the Spirit*, Minneapolis, Bethany Fellowship Inc., 1964, p. 99 ff.)

CHRIST ADOPTING CHILDREN

The adoption of children by Jesus Christ.
Ephesians 1:5, KJV

". . . the adoption of children by Jesus Christ. . . ." That phrase struck and startled me one day in my study of the Scriptures. I had been asked to christen two little ones, whom members of the congregation I served were taking into their families and into their hearts, and the text impressed me as delightfully relevant to the occasion. I had not thought before of Christ adopting children. I knew He was the friend of little children; I knew that, when on earth in physical presence, He had taken the little children in His arms and folded them in His bosom, but never before had it dawned on me that the Bible described Him as actually adopting children.

Yet there the statement stands, "the adoption of children by Jesus Christ." Paul is speaking, of course, about spiritual, not about natural, adoption. But I think that we may apply the words in the latter as well as in the former sense.

Why does Jesus adopt children?

1. **Because He was Himself an adopted Child.**

He was Mary's natural Son, but He was the adopted Son of Joseph.

2. **Because the adoption of children is one of the most Christ-like things anyone can do.**

3. **Because His adoption of children is for the children's highest good.**

Matthew 18:15-16; Matthew 18:19,20; 1 Corinthians 14:29

Perhaps it is because He is a member of the Holy Trinity that Jesus is so fond of the two's and three's. He has compassion on the crowds, but He has communion with the irreducibly minimal congregation.

There are three occurrences of the phrase *two or three* in the New Testament to which I wish for a short while to turn your attention.

1. Two or three for proof.

"If your brother sins against you, go and tell him his fault, between you and him alone. If he listens to you, you have gained your brother. But if he does not listen, take one or two others along with you, that every word may be confirmed by the evidence of two or three witnesses" (Matthew 18:15,16).

2. Two or three at prayer.

"If two of you agree on earth about anything they ask, it will be done for them by my Father in heaven. For where two or three are gathered in my name, there am I in the midst of them" (Matthew 18:19,20).

3. Two or three in prophecy.

"Let two or three prophets speak, and let the others weigh what is said" (1 Corinthians 14:29).

WITHOUT CHRIST

Without me ye can do nothing. John 15:5, KJV

In these words, Christ pictures a fearful possibility—
the possibility of a person being without Himself. "Without me": it is like depicting the world without the sun,
the year without the summer, life without health, and
that is what our life would be like without Him.

1. **Without Christ our past would be unpardonable.**

2. **Without Christ our present would be intolerable.**

3. **Without Christ our future would be impenetrable.**

Since we *have* Christ, our sinful past is forgiven, our
present is gladdened by His constant companionship and
our future is, in Carey's words, "as bright as the promises
of God." What a Christ!

THE CHRISTIAN AND THE CROSS

*Far be it from me to glory except in the cross of our Lord
Jesus Christ, by which the world has been crucified to
me, and I to the world.* Galatians 6:14

Thomas S. Kepler says that he seldom comes to a street
intersection without thinking of the cross. Joseph Plunkett
reacted similarly to the sight of a tree, and Thackeray to
that of a crane viewed against the background of a blood-
red sky. Intersection, tree, and crane set before them
visions of the cross.

81

Every true Christian is haunted by that vision. He stands related to the cross in three ways.

1. The Christian *at* the cross.
That is salvation.

2. The Christian *on* the cross.
That is sanctification.

It has been well said that no man can effectively preach *on* the cross unless he preaches *from* the cross.

3. The Christian *under* the cross.
That is submission, service, and sacrifice.

"An American businessman went to Oberammergau to witness the Passion Play. Enthralled by this great drama which depicts the story of the cross, he went backstage at the conclusion of the play to meet Mr. Anton Lang, who played the part of the Christus. Our American friend had equipped himself with an expensive camera which he was eager to use. Abruptly, he snapped the picture of Anton Lang. Then, looking about the stage for something more to photograph, he spotted in a corner the great cross which Mr. Lang had carried up the hill to Calvary in the play. Quickly turning to his wife, the tourist said, 'Here, dear, take my camera. I'm going over to lift up the cross. When I get it up on my shoulder, you snap my picture carrying the cross. Won't that be a novel and exciting photograph to send home to our friends in America?' He saw that Mr. Lang was frowning. 'You don't mind, Mr. Lang, do you?' he said. 'This is very unusual,' protested Mr. Lang. Before he could say more, however, the visitor had hurried over to the cross. He stooped to lift it on to his shoulder, but he could not move it one inch off the floor. That cross was made of heavy iron-oak beams. Amazed, he turned to Mr. Lang and said, 'Why, I thought it would be quite light. I fancied it would be hollow. Why do you carry a cross that is so terribly heavy?' Mr. Lang drew himself up to his full height and replied with dignity, 'Sir, if I did not feel the weight of His cross, I could not play His part.'" (Benjamin P. Browne, *Let There Be Light*, New Jersey, Fleming H. Revell Company, 1956, pp. 43, 44.)

THREE DIVINE RESPONSES TO PRAYER

2 Corinthians 12:8,9; 1 Samuel 1:27; 2 Corinthians 12:7

God responds to our prayers, broadly speaking, in three ways.

1. There are the things that we ask God for and that we don't get.

"Three times I besought the Lord about this, that it should leave me" (2 Corinthians 12:8).

2. There are the things that we ask God for and get.

"For this child I prayed; and the Lord has granted me my petition which I made to him" (1 Samuel 1:27).

3. There are the things that we get from God without asking.

"A thorn was given me in the flesh" (2 Corinthians 12:7).

The Abundance of Christ

I came that they may have life, and have it abundantly.
John 10:10 *Those who receive the abundance of grace.*
Romans 5:17 *By the power at work within us [He] is
able to do far more abundantly than all that we ask or
think.* Ephesians 3:20

That English word *abundance* has a picture at its
heart. It comes from the Latin. In that splendid speech
there are two expressions from which the English term
stems. One is *unda,* meaning a brook or stream; the other
is *abunda,* meaning a mighty rolling river. *Abundance*
springs from that root. It has within it the thought of the
overwhelming fullness, the swelling plenitude, of the
Amazon, the Danube, the Niger, the Mississippi.

Our texts bring before us the abundance of Christ.

1. **In Him there is abundance of life.**

2. **In Him there is abundance of grace.**

3. **In Him there is abundance of power.**

Rates of Exchange

What shall a man give in exchange? Mark 8:37, KJV

1. **Nothing for nothing.**

That is the pauper's experience.

In nothing is the realism of Jesus more manifest than
in the fact that He who said, "God so loved the world that

he gave his only Son" (John 8:16), also said, "No one gave him anything" (Luke 15:16).

2. Something for nothing.
That is the gambler's hope.

3. Something for something.
That is the businessman's *modus operandi.*

4. Everything for nothing.
That is the Christian offer.

God eternal is your home. Deuteronomy 33:27a, Translation by James Moffatt

1. A home is a place one is born into.

> Our birth is but a sleep and a forgetting:
> The soul that rises with us, our life's star,
>   Hath had elsewhere its setting,
>   And cometh from afar:
>   Not in entire forgetfulness,
>   And not in utter nakedness,
> But trailing clouds of glory do we come
>   From God, who is our home.
>
> William Wordsworth

2. A home is a place where one joins a family.

3. A home is a place where one is nourished and disciplined.

4. A home is a place where one receives shelter and protection.

5. A home is a place to which one invites one's friends.

THE HOLY SPIRIT IN EPHESIANS

Ephesians 1:13; 2:18; 3:16; 4:3

It is small wonder that Paul's Epistle to the Ephesians has a good deal to say about the Holy Spirit.

The first question ever addressed by the apostle to the dozen disciples, who formed the nucleus of the church at Ephesus, had to do with that subject. "Did you receive the Holy Spirit when you believed?" (Acts 19:2).

We know the sequel to that inquiry. The twelve Ephesians frankly admitted that they had not so much as heard of the Holy Spirit!

They certainly heard of Him afterwards from the Apostle Paul! In his letter to them, he speaks of the Spirit four times, employing four figures to set forth the truth concerning Him and His relations to the believers.

1. He is the seal of their security.
"In him you . . . were sealed with the promised Holy Spirit" (Ephesians 1:13).

2. He is the door of their access.
"For through him we both have access in one Spirit to the Father" (Ephesians 2:18).

3. He is the spring of their strength.

"That . . . he may grant you to be strengthened with might through his Spirit in the inner man" (Ephesians 3:16).

4. He is the groundwork of their unity.

"Eager to maintain the unity of the Spirit in the bond of peace" (Ephesians 4:3).

THE GODLESS

Having no hope and without God in the world.
Ephesians 2:12

There are many things in the world which, though we call them necessities, we can do without. We can do without wealth; we can do without health; we can do without family; we can do without friends; we can do without education; we can do without home.

But there is one thing—say rather one Person—we cannot do without, and that is God. As an old Welsh proverb succinctly expresses it: "Without God, without everything; God, and enough."

1. We cannot do without God providentially.

2. We cannot do without God redemptively.

3. We cannot do without God politically.

4. We cannot do without God morally.

5. We cannot do without God spiritually.

The Table of the Covenant

We . . . are one, for we all partake of the one bread.
1 Corinthians 10:17

A table has a strange way of drawing people together. Whether it be a banqueting table or a conference table, it exerts over us an extraordinary magnetic influence. This is true supremely of the communion table.

1. It draws us to Christ.

An old Puritan expressed a profound truth pithily when he said, "As God, Jesus Christ is everywhere; as resurrected Man, He can be anywhere."

His ubiquity does not destroy His human personality. He is present in spiritual totality wherever two or three assemble in His name. But if there is one place in the universe, apart from the eternal throne, where He is specially in evidence, it is at the celebration of this hallowed sacrament. The table draws us closer to Christ than anything else on earth.

2. It draws us as Christians nearer to one another.

Every unity conference should commence with the breaking of bread, for nothing reminds us more of solidarity in Christ than the levelling fellowship of the Eucharist. Here our divisions are seen in their real character—as rents in the body of Christ, not just tears in His robe. The communion table will do more than the conference table to foster interdenominational fellowship.

3. It draws us closer to the Christian departed.

Not to the rapping table of the spiritualists but to the table of the Lord do we resort, when seeking contact with those whom we have loved long since and lost awhile. Samuel John Stone was not indulging in empty rhetoric when in his immortal hymn, he wrote of the church.

> Yet she on earth hath union
>   With God the Three in One,
> And mystic sweet communion
>   With those whose rest is won:
> O happy ones and holy!
>   Lord, give us grace that we,
> Like them, the meek and lowly,
>   On high may dwell with Thee.

The Fire That Surprises Us

Do not be surprised at the fiery ordeal which comes upon you to prove you. 1 Peter 4:12

It is an incidental intimation of the essential goodness of life that fiery trials surprise us. C. S. Lewis strikingly names his spiritual autobiography *Surprised by Joy*. We are not usually surprised by *joy*. More often we take joy for granted. It is suffering that surprises us. When physical fire touches us, it shocks us; so do the fiery trials of the soul.

What does this fire do?

1. **It consumes.**

2. **It cleanses.**

3. **It comforts.**

4. **It conforms.**

The Master's Metaphors for the Holy Spirit

John 3:8; John 7:38,39; Luke 12:49

There are three major and vividly memorable metaphors which the Master used in seeking to set forth the nature and functions of the Holy Spirit.

He said that the Holy Spirit is:

1. Like wind in the mystery and liberty of His movements.

"The wind blows where it wills, and you hear the sound of it, but you do not know whence it comes or whither it goes; so it is with every one who is born of the Spirit" (John 3:8).

2. Like water in the refreshment and revitalization of His reception.

"He who believes in me, . . . 'Out of his heart shall flow rivers of living water.' . . . Now this he said about the Spirit, which those who believed in him were to receive; for as yet the Spirit had not been given, because Jesus was not yet glorified" (John 7:38,39).

3. Like fire in the consequences of His conflagration, combustion and consumption.

"I came to cast fire upon the earth; and would that it were already kindled!" (Luke 12:49).

Portrait of a Pair of Hands

She . . . works with willing hands. Proverbs 31:13

We are all familiar with Albrecht Durer's famous painting entitled "Praying Hands." The great artist has contrived to express by means of this manual portrayal the aspiration of a devout spirit. It is the portrait of a pair of hands.

Here in the last chapter of the Book of Proverbs we have a like picture. It is the picture of a good woman's hands. Let us look at it closely for a little.

We see that they are:

1. Toiling hands.

"With the fruit of her hands she plants a vineyard" (v.16).

"She puts her hands to the distaff, and her hands hold the spindle" (v.19).

You can tell a woman by her hands. Some women's hands are silken and smooth—the hands of the leisured lady. Some women's hands are horny and rough—the hands of the busy housewife. This good woman's hands were worn with toil.

2. Giving hands.

"She opens her hand to the poor" (v.20). The art of giving is the art of living.

3. Productive hands.

"Give her the fruit of her hands, and let her works praise her in the gates" (v.31).

OUR RELATIONS TO CHRIST

Ephesians 1:22; Colossians 1:18; John 3:29; Revelation 21:9; John 15:5; Romans 11:18; 1 Corinthians 3:11; Ephesians 2:21

1. He is the Head, we are the members.

"He has put all things under his feet and has made him the head over all things for the church, which is his body" (Ephesians 1:22,23).

"We are to grow up in every way into him who is the head, into Christ, from whom the whole body, joined and knit together by every joint with which it is supplied, when each part is working properly, makes bodily growth and upbuilds itself in love" (Ephesians 4:15,16).

"We are members of his body" (Ephesians 5:30).

"He is the head of the body, the church" (Colossians 1:18).

2. He is the Bridegroom, we are the bride.

"He who has the bride is the bridegroom; the friend of the bridegroom who stands and hears him, rejoices greatly at the bridegroom's voice; therefore this joy of mine is now full" (John 3:29).

"You have died to the law through the body of Christ, so that you may belong to another, to him who has been raised from the dead in order that we may bear fruit for God" (Romans 7:4).

"I betrothed you to Christ to present you as a pure bride to her one husband" (2 Corinthians 11:2).

"Come, and I will show you the Bride, the wife of the Lamb" (Revelation 21:9).

3. He is the Shepherd, we are the sheep.

"He who enters by the door is the shepherd of the sheep" (John 10:2).

"Tend my sheep" (John 21:16).

"Now may the God of peace who brought again from the dead our Lord Jesus, the great shepherd of the sheep, by the blood of the eternal covenant, equip you with everything good that you may do his will, working in you that which is pleasing in his sight, through Jesus Christ; to whom be glory for ever and ever. Amen" (Hebrews 13:20,21).

"You were straying like sheep, but have now returned to the Shepherd and Guardian of your souls" (1 Peter 2:25).

4. He is the Vine, we are the branches.

"I am the vine, you are the branches. He who abides in me, and I in him, he it is that bears much fruit, for apart from me you can do nothing" (John 15:5).

"If some of the branches were broken off, and you, a wild olive shoot, were grafted in their place to share the richness of the olive tree, do not boast over the branches. If you do boast, remember it is not you that support the root, but the root that supports you" (Romans 11:17,18).

5. He is the Foundation, we are the temple.

"According to the commission of God given to me, like a skilled master builder I laid a foundation, and another man is building upon it. Let each man take care how he builds upon it. For no other foundation can any one lay than that which is laid, which is Jesus Christ" (1 Corinthians 3:10,11).

"In whom the whole structure is joined together and grows into a holy temple in the Lord; in whom you also are built into it for a dwelling place of God in the Spirit" (Ephesians 2:21-2).

(James Sprunt, *Pithy Points,* London, George Stoneman, n.d., pp. 54,55).

THE HUNGRY CHRIST

In the morning, as he was returning to the city, he was hungry. Matthew 21:18 *He fasted forty days and forty nights, and afterward he was hungry.* Matthew 4:2 *I was hungry and you gave me food, . . . "Lord, when did we see thee hungry?"* Matthew 25:35,37

One of the strongest proofs of the real humanity of Jesus was that He hungered. He whose sun is forever ripening a harvest somewhere on this spinning ball which we call the earth; He who clothes the wide prairies with millions of square acres of heavy-headed grain; He on whose providential provision every living thing is pensioner—*He hungered!*

There is an ironical passage in the Psalms in which we

hear God crying, "If I were hungry, I would not tell you; for the world and all that is in it is mine" (Psalm 50:12). But Jesus *does* tell us that He is hungry.

Consider in succession our three texts, in which the hunger of Jesus is presented to us from different angles.

1. Hunger as a natural fact.

Doctors tell us that to be hungry in the morning is a sign of good health. Here is incidental evidence of the abounding health of the human Jesus. He was hungry in the morning!

2. Hunger with a moral motive.

> Forty days and forty nights
> > Thou wast fasting in the wild;
> Forty days and forty nights
> > Tempted, and yet undefiled.
> Let us Thy endurance share
> > And from earthly greed abstain;
> With Thee watching unto prayer,
> > With Thee strong to suffer pain.
>
> George Hunt Smyttan

3. Hunger as a spiritual passion.

"I was hungry."

Among those who have nothing to eat must be included our Lord Himself. He feels the hunger of every man as if it were His own. But deeper, infinitely deeper, than such vicarious physical hunger is His hunger for the souls of men.

And [God] gave to Moses, when he had made an end of speaking with him upon Mount Sinai, the two tables of the testimony, tables of stone, written with the finger of God. Exodus 31:18 *Jesus bent down and wrote with his finger on the ground.* John 8:6 *You show that you are a letter from Christ delivered by us, written not with ink but with the Spirit of the living God, not on tables of stone but on tablets of human hearts.* 2 Corinthians 3:3

One of the minor penalties of fame is to become the prey of the autograph hunter. Celebrities of every kind— sportsmen, actors, politicians, and the rest—are constantly beset on public occasions with people clamoring for a signature. It would be an interesting, and no doubt an illuminating psychological study, to consider what precisely it is which prompts this passion to possess specimens of the handwriting of notabilities.

There is, however, one autograph which is neither recognized nor valued as it should be—the autograph of God.

The Bible tells us that each of the Persons in the blessed Trinity supplies us with a specimen of His handwriting.

1. **We see the autograph of God the Father in creation.** Read Exodus 31:18.

2. **We see the autograph of God the Son in history.** Read John 8:6.

3. We see the autograph of God the Holy Spirit in human experience. Read 2 Corinthians 3:3.

CHRIST AND THE CROWDS

When he saw the crowds, he had compassion for them, because they were harassed and helpless, like sheep without a shepherd. Matthew 9:36

Matthew Arnold, the nineteenth century English man of letters, divided society into three classes and described what he alleged was happening to them in his day. He said that the contemporary social structure consisted of, "an upper class, materialized; a middle class, vulgarized; and a lower class, brutalized."

Let us see what Christ does to these three social groups.

1. He humanizes the upper classes.

Think of William Wilberforce, Lord Shaftesbury, C. T. Studd, Elizabeth Fry, Florence Nightingale, etc., and what they did for their fellows. That is what Christ can do to the upper classes.

2. He spiritualizes the middle classes.

Some years ago I attended a lunch-hour service in one of the great London churches. Next to me sat a businessman who, when the offering was taken, struggled to stuff without ostentation a wad of pound notes into the narrow neck of the collection bag. At the close, he wrung my hand warmly, although he was to me a total stranger, and, with eyes glistening, said, "Eternal values, my friend! Eternal values!"

That is what Christ can do to the middle classes.

3. He sensitizes the lower classes.

In California, I met a converted boxer who had once bidden fair to become world champion and had fought in the ring with Joe Louis, when he occupied that coveted position. He told me that, not long after giving his heart to Christ, he ran into a former boxing rival of his, whom at one time he had bitterly hated. Seeing him now, he was suddenly overcome with measureless compassion for him and had to restrain himself from throwing his arms round the other's neck. That is what Christ can do to the lower classes, and He does it because all of them He *evangelizes*.

WHAT FAITH DOES

Hebrews 11

Here we have faith defined by description; its nature revealed by its achievements; what it is, demonstrated by what it does.

1. Faith sees the invisible.

"Faith . . . is the conviction of things not seen" (v.1).

2. Faith does the impossible.

"Time would fail me to tell of Gideon, Barak, Samson, Jephthah, of David and Samuel and the prophets—who through faith conquered kingdoms, enforced justice, received promises, stopped the mouths of lions, quenched raging fire, escaped the edge of the sword, won strength out of weakness, became mighty in war, put foreign armies to flight" (vv.32-34).

3. Faith suffers the intolerable.

"Some were tortured, refusing to accept release, that they might rise again to a better life. Others suffered mocking and scourging, and even chains and imprisonment. They were stoned, they were sawn in two, they were killed with the sword; they went about in skins of sheep and goats, destitute, afflicted, ill-treated—wandering over deserts and mountains, and in dens and caves of the earth" (Hebrews vv.35-38).

4. Faith expects the unforeseeable.

"Now faith is the assurance of things hoped for" (v.1).

MORAL PLAYACTING

Matthew 6:1,2,5,6,16-18

It is no wonder that our Lord had so often on His lips the word *hypocrite*. As a matter of fact, nobody but He is recorded by the New Testament as having used it. The Greek term *hupokrites*, of which our English word is almost an exact transcription, means literally *actor*—one who wears a mask and plays a part.

To most of their contemporaries the religious leaders of Christ's day appeared good and godly men. Their conduct seemed exemplary in the extreme. Accepting

99

them at their face value, the people were completely taken in by the pious pretence.

Not so Jesus. With the piercing insight of omniscience, He penetrated beneath their moral mask. His probing gaze, like the eye of some powerful X-ray camera, saw right through their clerical camouflage and detected what they really were beyond the image which they were concerned to present to the public.

Stripping the masks of piety from their false faces, He showed them up for what they truly were—actors, not real men.

Among other things, He charged them particularly with hypocrisy in three directions.

1. **He charged them with hypocrisy in their praying.**

"When you pray, you must not be like the hypocrites; for they love to stand and pray in the synagogues and at the street corners, that they may be seen by men. Truly, I say to you, they have their reward. But when you pray, go into your room and shut the door and pray to your Father who is in secret; and your Father who sees in secret will reward you" (Matthew 6:5,6).

2. **He charged them with hypocrisy in their fasting.**

"When you fast, do not look dismal, like the hypocrites, for they disfigure their faces that their fasting may be seen by men. Truly, I say to you, they have their reward. But when you fast, anoint your head and wash your face, that your fasting may not be seen by men but by your Father who is in secret; and your Father who sees in secret will reward you" (Matthew 6:16-18).

3. He charged them with hypocrisy in their giving.

"Beware of practicing your piety before men in order to be seen by them; for then you will have no reward from your Father who is in heaven. Thus, when you give alms, sound no trumpet before you, as the hypocrites do in the synagogues and in the streets, that they may be praised by men. Truly, I say to you, they have their reward. But when you give alms, do not let your left hand know what your right hand is doing, so that your alms may be in secret; and your Father who sees in secret will reward you" (Matthew 6:1,2).

THE FINGER OF GOD

When I look at thy heavens, the work of thy fingers. Psalm 8:3 *And [God] gave to Moses, when he had made an end of speaking with him upon Mount Sinai, the two tables of the testimony, tables of stone, written with the finger of God.* Exodus 31:18 *Immediately the fingers of a man's hand appeared and wrote on the plaster of the wall of the king's palace, opposite the lampstand; and the king saw the hand as it wrote.* Daniel 5:5 *Jesus bent down and wrote with his finger on the ground.* John 8:6

Without interpreting the imagery in any crude anthropomorphic manner, we can all see the fitness of the figure, *the finger of God.*

In our four texts we see respectively:

1. The finger of God in creation.

2. **The finger of God in the commandments.**

3. **The finger of God in condemnation.**

4. **The finger of God in compassion.**

BREAD

On the first day of the week, when we were gathered together to break bread. Acts 20:7

Bread! Looked at with the eye of imagination, it is a miracle in matter, a composition of granulated grace. As W. J. Rowlands writes in *The Suburban Christ,* "A loaf is a wonderful thing. It is a mystery. It is a providence. It is the result of the cooperation of man, nature, and God. It is the symbol of the unity and partnership of the three."

1. **It takes God to make bread.**

   There is a familiar story about a minister who, walking one day along a country road, met a boy carrying on his head a basket of loaves. "Hello, young man," said the minister. "Where did you get the bread?" "From the baker, sir," replied the lad. "And where did the baker get the bread?" "From the miller, sir." "And where did the miller get the bread?" "From the farmer, sir." "And where did the farmer get the bread?" "From the seedsman sir." "And where did the seedsman get the bread?" Here the boy came to a halt. He seemed unable to pursue his logic any further. For a moment or two he was silent. Then his face brightened and, touching his cap, he said: "From God, sir!" Just so! As Maltbie D. Babcock has written in his poem, "Give Us This Day Our Daily Bread":

Back of the loaf is the snowy flour,
Back of the flour the mill;
Back of the mill is the wheat and the shower
And the sun, and the Father's will.

(Ian Macpherson, *God's Middleman*, London, Epworth Press, 1965, pp. 135-36.)

2. It takes nature to make bread.

If nature did not respond or were not amenable to the processes of agriculture, and if the surface of the earth were all solid rock with no soil, the production of bread would be impossible. It takes a universe to make a loaf. The seed, the soil, the rain, the sun—each has its part to play, and without any one of them the sequence of productivity would be fatally interrupted, and the making of bread ruled out of the realm of possibility.

3. It takes man to make bread.

Bread does not grow on bushes. It does not fall like snow. It has to be painstakingly prepared by human hands.

I never see a baker in his shop without wanting to raise my hat to him. He is the priest of the family table, and but for his services the human household could not long continue. So it is really a matter of the baker or the undertaker.

DISCERNING THE LORD'S BODY

Anyone who eats and drinks without discerning the body eats and drinks judgment upon himself. 1 Corinthians 11:29

There are four ways in which Christ's body was, is, or will be discerned:

1. Some saw Christ's body in the flesh.

"Even though we once regarded Christ from a human point of view, we regard him thus no longer" (2 Corinthians 5:16).

2. Some see Christ's body in the Church.

"He has put all things under his feet and has made him the head over all things for the church, which is His body (Ephesians 1:22,23).

3. Some see Christ's body in the sacramental bread.

"The bread which we break, is it not a participation in the body of Christ?" (1 Corinthians 10:16).

4. All will see Christ's body in its dazzling glory.

"Every eye will see him" (Revelation 1:7).

IN THE POTTER'S HOUSE

The word that came to Jeremiah from the Lord: "Arise, and go down to the potter's house, and there I will let you hear my words." So I went down to the potter's house, and there he was working at his wheel. And the vessel he was making of clay was spoiled in the potter's hand, and he reworked it into another vessel, as it seemed good to the potter to do. Jeremiah 18:1-4

In his engaging book *The Gift of Wings*, John Macbeath tells of a bell in Dunblane Cathedral, Scotland, with this inscription, "I was founded in Edinburgh in 1612, by the care of William Blaikwood, Bailie of Dunblane, and stayed so in my exercise until 1657, when I was broken by the unskillful direction and handling of some men. But by the care and expense of Henri Blaikwood, William's son, I am founded again at Brimin, 1660."

The fate of that cathedral bell is like the fate of the vessel that Jeremiah saw when he went down to the potter's house. It may be summed up by three words:

1. **Formed.**

"He was working at his wheel."

2. **Deformed.**

"The vessel he was making of clay was spoiled in the potter's hand."

> For I remember stopping by the way
> To watch a Potter thumping his wet Clay:

And with its all-obliterated Tongue
It murmur'd—"Gently, Brother, gently, pray!"

Edward Fitzgerald, Omar Khayyam

3. Re-formed.

"He reworked it into another vessel."

UP WITH THE LARK

Be ready in the morning. Exodus 34:2

This divine command can be applied in four connections.

1. Be ready in the morning of life.

2. Be ready in the morning of each day.

John Henry Jowett, one of the most popular preachers of modern times, used to apply to preachers a question asked in Job: "Hast thou commanded the morning?" He held that to miss the morning in sermon preparation is to miss the day, "the pure fresh hours of the morning when the soul of the day is at its best."

3. Be ready in the morning of opportunity.

4. Be ready in the morning of eternity.

The brave Scottish Covenanter, Donald Cargill, standing on the scaffold in the Grassmarket of Edinburgh, where thousands had gathered to witness his execution, cried, "Now for the morning and the King's face. No more night and no more darkness."

She gave birth to her first-born son and wrapped him in swaddling cloths, and laid him in a manger, because there was no place for them in the inn. Luke 2:7 *The soldiers arrayed . . . him in a purple robe.* John 19:2 *They . . . put his own clothes on him.* Matthew 27:31

In each of these texts mention is made of the clothing of Christ

1. The clothes His mother gave Him.

May C. Smith thus describes the swaddling cloths in which the infant Christ was wrapped: "A broad strip of cloth, six inches by nine feet, wound around the bodies of babies in Palestine."

2. The clothes the soldiers gave Him.

"He was thus mocked," says Matthew Henry, "not in His own clothes, but in another's, to signify that He suffered not for His own sin."

3. The clothes His friends gave Him.

"When the soldiers had crucified Jesus they took his garments and made four parts, one for each soldier; also his tunic. But the tunic was without seam, woven from top to bottom; so they said to one another, 'Let us not tear it, but cast lots for it to see whose it shall be'" (John 19:23,24).

I wonder whose nimble fingers wove that lovely robe. Were they His mother's? Mary Magdalene's? Mary of Bethany's? I don't know; but I know this—however beautiful that garment was, it could not compare in loveliness with the robe He wove for her on the dark loom of the cross.

God at Work

The heavens are the work of thy hands. Hebrews 1:10
The working of his great might which he accomplished in Christ when he raised him from the dead. Ephesians 1:19,20 *They went forth and preached everywhere, while the Lord worked with them and confirmed the message by the signs that attended it.* (Mark 16:20)

There is an oft-quoted passage in J. Anthony Froude's classic biography of Thomas Carlyle in which the author describes how he and Carlyle were once discussing the woes and wrongs of the world. "I can only believe in a God who does something," said Froude. Whereupon the sage of Chelsea was suddenly roused to a mood of high tragedy. "He does nothing!" Carlyle broke out bitterly. "He does nothing! He looks on and does nothing!"

Now that is a statement at violent variance with the facts. The concept of an unemployed God is completely contrary to the Christian revelation of His character. Sometimes in our streets we see posted up beside that eternal hole in the road the notice: *Caution. Men at work.* Usually that is an exaggeration. But the New Testament puts up a placard: *God at work* and that is no exaggeration. An eccentric preacher I know has a sermon on Isaiah 52:10, "The Lord has bared his holy arm," to which he gives the quaint title, "God with His Sleeves Rolled up." That is the picture of God which the Bible presents.

1. **It shows us God at work in creation** in Hebrews 1:10.

2. **It shows us God at work in the historic career of Christ** in Ephesians 1:19, 20.

3. **It shows us God at work in the mission and service of the church** in Mark 16:20.

How Leaves Fade

We all fade like a leaf. Isaiah 64:6

Leaves fade:

1. **Gradually.**

2. **Silently.**

3. **Differently.**

4. **Characteristically.**

5. **Preparedly.**

(John A. Kern. Quoted by G. G. Atkins, *The Undiscovered Country*, New York, Fleming H. Revell, 1922, p. 287.)

Earmarked

When you buy a Hebrew slave, he shall serve six years, and in the seventh he shall go out free, for nothing. If he comes in single, he shall go out single; if he comes in married, then his wife shall go out with him. If his master gives him a wife and she bears him sons or daughters, the wife and her children shall be her master's and he shall go out alone. But if the slave plainly says, "I love my master, my wife, and children; I will not go out free," then his master shall bring him to God, and he shall bring him to the door or the doorpost; and his master shall bore his ear through with an awl; and he shall serve him for life. Exodus 21:2-6

According to old Jewish custom, a slave whose time of servitude was up could, of his own free will, stay on with his master. In that case, the judges of the city, in the presence of the people, bored a hole with an awl in the man's ear. The bored ear was the sign of voluntary service; hence the word *earmarked*.

All God's servants are earmarked in three ways.

1. **They are earmarked in the sense that they listen to the voice of God in their own consciences.**

2. **They are earmarked in that they hearken to the Word of God in the Bible.**

3. **They are earmarked in that they attend to the cry of sinning, sorrowing humanity.**

FORGIVENESS

But there is forgiveness with thee, that thou mayest be feared. Psalm 130:4

1. Some people are not aware of the need for forgiveness.

Said the dying Horatio Nelson, "Hardy, I have not been a great sinner."

Henry David Thoreau said to his aunt, who had bidden him make his peace with God, "I did not know that we had ever quarrelled."

2. Some people forgive themselves too easily.

It is the mark of royal souls that they find it hard to pardon themselves. Think of Samuel Johnson standing bareheaded in the rain in Lichfield market place as a penance for a misdemeanor as a boy.

3. Some people cannot forgive themselves.

4. Some people seek forgiveness at the wrong source.

"Suppose that I have done you an injury and that, conscious of my fault, I go to someone else—a third party not at all concerned with the matter—and suppose that I confess and apologize to *him* and ask *him* to forgive me. What would you say if I did that? You would say: 'What has *he* got to do with it? He can't put things right, because he has nothing to put right. I alone can do that, since it was to me that the wrong was done!' Obviously! Only he against whom the offence has been committed possesses the power and the prerogative to pardon. Sin is ultimately an offence against God, and none but God can forgive it." (Ian Macpherson, *None other Name*, London, Epworth Press, 1946, p. 48.)

5. Some people wisely recognize that only God can forgive sin.

The Head and the Body

He is the head of the body, the church. Colossians 1:18

1. A body belongs exclusively to its head.

It is strictly not transferable! *Heart* transplants but not *head* transplants!

2. A body is largely identified by its head.

In itself, it may have marks of identification, but it is truly recognizable only in relation to its head.

3. A body normally derives its nourishment from the head.

There are artificial means of feeding it which bypass the usual channels of assimilation, but the natural way of partaking of food is via the head.

4. A body, if in good health, responds perfectly to its head.

Failure to do so with alacrity is evidence that something is wrong.

5. A body finds its avenue of expression chiefly in the head.

It can express itself to some extent by means of gestures, and the like, but its main mode of communication is the head.

Apply all this to Christ and His church.

The Four Voices

I am who I am. Exodus 3:14 *By the grace of God I am what I am.* 1 Corinthians 15:10

Paul could say, "I am what I am," because there is One who describes Himself as "I am who I am."
There are four voices a Christian man may hear in his own soul.

1. **"I am not what I used to be."**
That is the voice of memory.

2. **"I am not what I ought to be."**
That is the voice of conscience.

3. **"I am not what I hope to be."**
That is the voice of aspiration.

4. **"By the grace of God I am what I am."**
That is the voice of the Christian consciousness.

Rags

All our righteousnesses are as filthy rags Isaiah 64:6, KJV

Reading that text makes one rub one's eyes. Surely there is something wrong with it! Surely what we have here is a translator's slip or a printer's error! Surely the sentence should run, "All our unrighteousnesses, (not our righteousnesses) are as filthy rags."

But the rendering is right. This is no copyist's mistake, no editor's oversight, no printer's blunder: this is the authentic Word of God. "Our righteousnesses," the best things we have ever done, the finest moral achievements we have to our credit, are in God's eyes but filthy rags.

1. Rags are things that were once good clothes.
Nothing ever *starts* as rags. So, too, we are in a sense born innocent.

2. Rags are never becoming.
It is said of some that they look glorious even in rags, but that is a compliment seldom borne out by the facts.

3. Rags betoken poverty.
As Spurgeon said, the most eloquent beggar is not he with the oiliest tongue, but he whose tatters have a tongue.

4. Rags are no reliable form of dress.
They cannot confidently be counted upon to cover one. One never knows when they are going to burst at the seams, or rend at some threadbare patch, and leave one naked and cold.

5. Rags urgently require replacement.
There is a true story about a little lad, destitute and in rotten rags, who was being stripped of them prior to being clad in fine clothes. The boy had grown to like the rags, and wept as they were being peeled off him. "But they are all my very own!" he cried. Aren't we a bit like that spiritually? Haven't we grown to love the rags of our own righteousness? And aren't we incredibly reluctant to put on the garments of grace?

THREE WAYS OF LIVING

Make me to know thy ways, O Lord. Psalm 25:4

An old lady, setting out by sea from England to Australia, asked the captain of the vessel on which she was voyaging what route he proposed to take. "Well, madam," he replied, pulling a map from his pocket and spreading it out for the old lady to examine, "there are three possibilities. This is a short cut. It is the way I should prefer to go. This is another route which is by far the most interesting. But this, madam, is the way the directors of the company who own the ship want me to take. And I'm going that way!"

There are three ways one may take as one travels through life.

1. There is the way we ourselves naturally want to go.
"There is a way which seems right to a man" (Proverbs 14:12).

2. There is the way other people would fain persuade us to take.
"The way of sinners" (Psalm 1:1).

3. There is the way the Lord wants us to take, and we are going that way!
"This is the way, walk in it" (Isaiah 30:21).

Jesus the pioneer and perfecter of our faith, who for the joy that was set before him endured the cross. Hebrews 12:2

It is a law of life that those who will not endure shall not enjoy. As the old proverb has it, there are no gains without pains. And, we might almost add, there are no pleasures without pains. Both enduring and enjoying are parts of man's lot. In our facing of the future, therefore, it is immensely important that we get them into proper perspective. Not many do.

1. **Some see only the *enduring* and forget the *enjoying*, and that makes them sad.**

2. **Some see only the *enjoying* and forget the *enduring*, and that makes them shallow.**

3. **Jesus, and all His true disciples, see both, and *endure* that they may *enjoy*.**

> Joy and woe are woven fine,
> A clothing for the soul divine;
> And when this we rightly know,
> Through the world we safely go.
>
> William Blake

Light and Sight

Awake, O sleeper, and arise from the dead, and Christ shall give you light. Ephesians 5:14

You cannot give light to a sleeping person until he awakens. His body may be bathed in solar radiance, and the sunlight may be falling full on his face, but as long as he slumbers, you cannot give him light.

Spiritually speaking, the same applies. Christ is the Light of the world, the Sun of the soul, but until the sinner awakens from his sleep, Christ cannot give him light. Hence the startling relevance of our text. In this regard there are four sorts of people.

1. Some are asleep in the dark.

They are the sinners in pagan lands—people who have never been enlightened by the Christian revelation, nor visited by the pure light of the Gospel.

2. Some are asleep in the light.

They are the sinners who, amid the blaze of Christian truth in our so-called Christian countries, nevertheless remain oblivious of it and even unconscious of it.

3. Some are awake in the dark.

They are like Peter when his prison has suddenly illuminated. He woke, and the dungeon flamed with light. Peter, while asleep, had been oblivious of his cell, his chain, and his guards. Now he saw his position.

4. Some are awake in the light.

They are those who have savingly responded to the rousing challenge of the text, "Awake, O sleeper, . . . and Christ shall give you light."

Between the vestibule and the altar let the priests, the ministers of the Lord, weep and say, "Spare thy people, O Lord, and make not thy heritage a reproach, a byword among the nations. Why should they say among the peoples, 'Where is their God?' " Joel 2:17

A distinguished American college president once preached the ordination sermon when his son was being inducted as a Christian minister. Among much capital counsel which the father gave was this, "Keep close to God. Keep close to man. Bring God and man together."

It would be hard to better that advice. There is no finer position for a minister of Christ to occupy than that between the throne and the throng, between the vestibule and the altar, between a loving and holy God and rebellious, sinful men.

1. **Keep close to God.**

2. **Keep close to man.**

3. **Bring God and man together.**

That is a perfect epitome of the minister's task.

THE FATHER'S LOVE FOR US

The Father himself loves [philei] you. John 16:27

It is most important to stress that we ought not to take our idea of the Fatherhood of God from our observation or experience of the fatherhood of man. Human fatherhood is so often a sheer travesty of the Fatherhood divine.

"A Sunday School teacher was once shocked," says Michael Bruce, "by the violence with which a small boy rejected belief in God. 'Don't you want a heavenly Father?' she asked. 'No,' he replied decidedly, 'I don't want no heavenly Father. My Dad beats me, and that's enough!'" (*No Empty Creed*, Derby, England, Peter Smith, 1964, p. 85.)

I remember a blind girl coming to me many years ago in much distress of mind and putting to me one of the hardest questions I have ever been called upon to answer. "Should I leave home?" she asked. "My father is making sexual assaults upon me which, because of my sightlessness, I cannot escape!"

Not long ago the newspapers printed the terrible story of a father who, in a fit of temper, had broken his own baby's back.

Fatherhood! No! Do not let us take our ideas of fatherhood from man but from God. That is how Paul construes the case. "I bow my knees," he writes, "before the Father, from whom every family in heaven and on earth is named" (Ephesians 3:14,15).

Observe that:

1. A father's love is a love that is hurt by the faults, failures and follies of his family.

2. A father's love is a love which will do everything in its power for the well-being of his family.

3. A father's love is a love which will place all it possesses at the disposal of his family.

"Son, you are always with me, and all that is mine is yours" (Luke 15:31).

How Old Are You?

And Pharaoh said unto Jacob, How old art thou? Genesis 47:8, KJV

How old are you? We would probably call that a rude and impertinent question—the sort of question that one addresses only to small boys, or to people whom we know to be rather proud of their age, for one reason or another. Were the interrogation made of a representative group in this congregation, there would certainly be a wide variety of replies. There are, however, several broad answers that can be given to it.

1. "How old are you?" "Older than I once was."

2. "How old are you?" "Older than I am willing to think of."

3. "How old are you?" "Old enough to know better."

4. "How old are you?" "Old enough to become a committed Christian."

(Andrew Henderson, *The Measure of a Man*, Paisley, Scotland, Alexander Gardner, 1897, pp. 191-204.)

A Man Worth Listening To

You should have listened to me. Acts 27:21

There are several possible reasons why Paul was not listened to on that occasion. For one thing, he was small of stature—a mere midget, it is said—and those who had no means of measuring his mind might have thought him not worth listening to because of his diminutiveness. For another thing, he probably did not seem a practical man. It is true that he was a tentmaker, and so accustomed to using his hands, (every Jewish boy was compelled to learn a trade); but the whole bent of his being was towards scholarship. Practical men, such as the shipmaster and the centurion, tend to treat men of the scholarly type with a certain haughty contempt when the bookworms turn and try to take a hand in material affairs. For a third thing, Paul was a prisoner, and who gives much for the opinions of an accused man? For yet another thing, Paul was a Jew, a member of a subjugated people occupying a mere eyebrow of land on the eastern seaboard of the Mediterranean. What did it matter what a landlubber like this Jew thought about a critical situation at sea?

For all these reasons, Paul was not listened to. Had he been listened to, shipwreck would have been avoided.

1. **Wise men cannot always get the hearing they merit.**

2. Those who refuse to listen to wise men commonly live to regret it.

3. The wise man usually gets his chance at last.

A Question of Supplies

What have you in the house? 2 Kings 4:2

This is an inquiry of pressing importance to every housewife. "What have you in the house?" Constantly recurring demands are made on the domestic resources. Is there anything in reserve? Or is there immediate need for replenishment? What is in the house?

Let us draw out in four directions the question of our text.

1. **What have you in the house of your heart?**

2. **What have you in the house which is your natural home?**

3. **What have you in the house which we call the church?** What have you made your very own of its teaching and experience, work and witness?

4. **What have you in that house, not made with hands, which is to be your dwelling place forever?**

The Sin of Prayerlessness

God forbid that I should sin against the Lord in ceasing to pray for you. 1 Samuel 12:23, KJV

It is important to recognize that sin can be of two kinds. Sin consists either in the doing of what I know to be wrong—"Sin is the transgression of the law" (1 John 3:4, KJV); or sin is the failure to do what I know to be right—"To him that knoweth to do good, and doeth it not, to him it is sin" (James 4:17, KJV). We call these, theologically, sins of commission and sins of omission. Both are sins. It is questionable whether it is worse to be a man who does the worst, or one who fails to do the best. Possibly such are equally sinners in the sight of God.

One of the most common, most serious, sins in Christian living is the sin of prayerlessness.

1. **Prayerlessness is sin because by prayerlessness the cross of Christ is despised.**

2. **Prayerlessness is sin because by it the church of Christ is deprived.**

3. **Prayerlessness is sin because by it the cause of Christ is defeated.**

(George B. Duncan in *More Sermons I should Like to have Preached*, Edit. by Ian Macpherson, London, Epworth Press, 1967, p. 28 ff.)

FACETS OF THE FAITH

Romans 1:16; Romans 2:16; 2 Thessalonians 2:14
The Gospel of Christ has three aspects.

1. **It it historical.**

"I am not ashamed of the gospel" (Romans 1:16).

2. **It is personal.**
"According to my gospel" (Romans 2:16).

3. **It is social.**
"To this he called you through our gospel" (2 Thessalonians 2:14).

The Right End of the Stick

He disarmed the principalities and powers and made a public example of them, triumphing over them in him. Colossians 2:15

George Bernard Shaw, that expert in verbal shock tactics, once said that men crucified Jesus on a stick, but that He somehow managed to get the right end of it. It probably is true that the gallows to which the Roman legionaries nailed Christ was little better than two sticks— at any rate, two rough logs. Art has pictured Christ on a carved cross, a finely-joinered gibbet with smoothly planed beams and symmetrical shape, but that is almost certainly a romantic misrepresentation. The timbers of the holy tree were likely pretty much what they had been in the woods before they were cut down, a couple of crude boughs. Yes, it can almost be maintained with literal truth that they crucified Christ on a stick.

It is also true that He got the right end of it. Presumably, the point of the figure is that one takes the thing that is beating one and uses it as an instrument of one's own purpose.

That is precisely what Christ did with His cross. He got the right end of that stick and turned defeat into resounding victory. By His cross He conquered.

1. He got the right end of the stick where His human foes were concerned.

They thought they had finished Him. Having skewered Him on Calvary, they dusted their hands, congratulating themselves on a tough and tricky job well done. To get Him pinned up there without starting a popular uprising in His favor was, they told themselves, no mean achievement. Now He was dead and gone, and that was that!

But it wasn't!

2. He got the right end of the stick where sin was concerned.

It looked as if evil was the mightiest thing in the universe, and as if goodness, even absolute goodness, was completely at its mercy. It seemed as if sin were sovereign, but Christ got the right end of the stick and struck sin a fatal blow with His cross.

3. He got the right end of the stick where death was concerned.

To all appearances death had falsified Christ's claims forever. He had declared Himself "the Resurrection and the Life" and if ever there was an ironic moment in human history it was when He, who had professed to be Life and Resurrection, hung a limp corpse with glazed eyes on a gallows!

But things are not always what they seem. In this sense, likewise, our Lord got the right end of the stick, and He who had proclaimed Himself the Life when alive, proved Himself the Resurrection when dead.

THE RIVER OF GOD

There is a river whose streams make glad the city of God. Psalm 46:4

Three things about a river call for special comment here.

1. **The flowing of the river.**

You don't have to make a river flow. Its nature is to do just that.

    a. It flows descendingly.

    b. It flows extendingly.

    c. It flows unendingly.

        You recall the old fabulist's story of the simpleton who sat down on the bank of a river and who, when asked what he was doing there, replied, "I am waiting for the river to pass so that I can get across."

2. **The fertilizing of the river.**

3. **The force of the river.**

I bow my knees before the Father, . . . that . . . he may grant you to be . . . filled with all the fulness of God. Ephesians 3:14,16,19

"Man," says Billy Graham, "was not made for emptiness." Adam C. Welch agrees. "You've got to fill a man with something," he declares.

1. Man was meant to be filled *physically,* and so there is food.

2. Man was meant to be filled *mentally,* and so there is truth.

3. Man was meant to be filled *emotionally,* and so there is friendship.

4. Man was meant to be filled *spiritually,* and so there is God.

THE QUEST FOR GOD

Seek the Lord while he may be found, call upon him while he is near. Isaiah 55:6

Everything of worth in this world has to be sought for. Only the valueless lies ready to hand. Gold is not exposed on the surface of the planet for man to pick up casually: it is hidden in the heart of the earth, as if even Nature itself prized it highly, and has to be dug up, filtered from the sludge of muddy rivers, and smelted from the solid quartz. Pearls do not float on the face of the sea: they are embedded within the shells of oysters in the depth of the ocean, and have to be got with great hardship and hazard.

> Are there not . . .
> Two points in the adventure of the diver,
> One—when, a beggar, he prepares to plunge,
> One—when, a prince, he rises with his pearl?
>
> Robert Browning

Learning is not acquired by looking at the binding of books in a library: it is only come by at colossal cost. Everything of worth in this world has to be sought for.

So it is with the values of the other world. It is true, in one sense, that heaven can be had for the asking and that God is given away. But, if we are truly to find God, we must ask in faith for the revelation and we must seek Him with patient intensity. "You will seek me and find me; when you seek me with all your heart" (Jeremiah 29:13). That is the condition, and that is the cost.

1. Some seek God in the world without.

That is the way of naturism.

2. Some seek God in the world within.

That is the way of mysticism. The trouble with mysticism, as the wit said, is that it begins in *mist* and ends in *schism*.

3. Some seek God in the world above.

That is the way of evangelicalism. Once we discover

that true God, or rather are found of Him, we encounter Him in the world around us and in the world within.

The fact is, the best things never become ours unless we go in quest of them, and the best quest of all is the quest for God.

The Room of Pictures

Have you seen what the elders of . . . Israel are doing in the dark, every man in his room of pictures? Ezekiel 8:12

A man's true worship, it has been said, is not the worship which he performs in the public temple, but that which he offers in the little private chapel where nobody goes but himself. It is this latter worship, rather than the other, from which his life takes its color.

Whom or what do we worship in this private chapel?

1. **Some worship there an idol called** *Things.*

Whatever our professed political allegiance, human nature being what it is, the possession of things, and particularly the worship of things, turns us into conservatives. Watch! a dog becomes a conservative when you give him a bone.

2. **Some worship there the little god** *Self.*

Of the worship of this idol, in one way or another, we all stand convicted. Someone once described Benjamin Disraeli as a self-made man who worshipped his creator. Too many of us are like that. If you were to peer into the darkness of that private chapel where the real devotions of our lives are conducted, you would see us worshipping that miserable petty image.

3. **Some worship there the true and living God whose name is Christ.**

D. L. Moody fathered the familiar aphorism that character is what a man does in the dark. It would be equally true to say that what a man does in the dark depends upon what he worships in the dark. The hardest and most determinative thing in the Christian life is really to set Christ on the throne in that inner shrine of human personality. He will not *take* that throne: we must *give* it to Him. When we do, life swings into its proper orbit, for it has found its true focus.

Henry Drummond tells the now well-known story of a woman whose son went up to the university. When visiting him in his room, she was shocked to find the walls covered with obscene pictures. Being a wise parent, she did not protest against the pictures nor show her feeling about them in any way. Instead she bought a picture of Christ and asked him to put that up in his room. He did. When next his mother called to see him, she was secretly delighted to discover that what she had expected to happen had in fact taken place. The picture of Christ had made impossible the display of all the others. Only the pure features of Jesus were to be seen on the wall.

THE CHRISTIAN'S TEACHERS

1 Timothy 1:20; Philippians 4:11; Ephesians 4:11; Ephesians 4:20

How much we owe, naturally speaking, to our teachers! Very probably, in our childhood we did not much appreciate them. We found them boring, authoritarian, and restrictive. Yet how greatly impoverished we should be today, had we not learned the lessons they gave us! Think for a little of the Christian's teachers. Thomas Arnold, Bronson Alcott, and William Temple were mere educational amateurs in comparison with them.

1. Satan can be the Christian's teacher.

"By rejecting conscience, certain persons have made shipwreck of their faith, among them Hymenaeus and Alexander, whom I have delivered to Satan that they may learn not to blaspheme" (1 Timothy 1:19,20).

2. Experience can be the Christian's teacher.

"I have learned, in whatever state I am, to be content. I know how to be abased, and I know how to abound; in any and all circumstances I have learned the secret of facing plenty and hunger, abundance and want" (Philippians 4:11,12).

3. Other Christians, particularly Christian ministers, can be the Christian's teachers.

"His gifts were that some should be . . . teachers" (Ephesians 4:11).

4. The Christian's supreme teacher is Christ.

"You did not so learn Christ!" (Ephesians 4:20).

They offered him wine mingled with myrrh; but he did not take it. Mark 15:23

One of the clamant evils of our day is dope addiction. Our times have been characterized by many names—the Atomic Age, the Age of Revolution, the Scientific Age, and so on. Isabel Leighton has come as close to comprehensiveness as any, in describing it as the Aspirin Age.

Nor is it merely coincidental that the generation which Karl Marx has taught to believe that religion is the opiate of the people, is turning more than any other to opiates as a means of escaping from the implications of being religionless.

Jesus on the cross declined dope. They offered Him a medicated draught to dull His senses and ease His pain, but He refused it.

So will every true Christian. When life threatens to prove too much for him, he will turn not to the illusory aids of the pill box, but to the Pentecostal power which God pours into the souls of those who ask for divine reinforcement.

Dope is of two major kinds, stimulant and sedative, producing, in the one case, an artificial sense of adequacy and, in the other, a spurious feeling of relaxation.

Power and rest! Christ offers both, and the real things, not false substitutes.

1. There are the stimulating galvanizers
a. Alcohol
b. Heroin, etc.

Christ offers something infinitely better in that direction. "Do not get drunk with wine, for that is debauchery; but be filled with the Spirit" (Ephesians 5:18).

"These men are not drunk, as you suppose, since it is only the third hour of the day; but this is what was spoken by the prophet Joel: 'And in the last days it shall be, God declares, that I will pour out my Spirit upon all flesh' " (Acts 2:15-17).

2. There are the stupefying tranquilizers.
a. Aspirin.

Someone has said that nowadays man's story can be summed up in terms of three tablets—school tablet, aspirin tablet, stone tablet.

b. Phenobarbital.

When anesthetics were first introduced they were violently opposed on moral grounds. Happily, that controversy is over.

Samuel Johnson, the English philosopher and litterateur, when told by his physician that recovery was impossible and when asked if he would care to have something administered to alleviate his pain, replied, "I will take no opiate. I have prayed that I may render up my soul to God unclouded."

That was noble, but nobody now queries the ethics of anesthesia.

This applies, of course, only to situations where suffering, mental or physical, is intolerable. In ordinary life such tranquilizers should not be necessary. Christ can supply that basic human need. "Come to me," He says, "all who labor and are heavy laden, and I will give you rest. Take my yoke upon you, and learn from me; for I am gentle and lowly in heart, and you will find rest for your souls. For my yoke is easy, and my burden is light" (Matthew 11:28,29).

3. There is the Pentecostal vitalizer.

In David Wilkerson's book *The Cross and the Switchblade*, there is an immensely significant passage in which he describes how he interrogated several young people who had been delivered by Christ from dope addiction. He writes:

> I spoke to Nicky, who had been taking goof balls and smoking marijuana. I asked him when it was that he felt he had victory over his old way of life. Something tremendous had happened to him, he said, at the time

of his conversion on the street corner. He had been introduced at that time to the love of God, but it wasn't until later that he knew he had complete victory.

"And when was that, Nicky?"

"At the time of my baptism in the Holy Spirit."

THREE KINDS OF PEACE

Ezekiel 13:10; John 14:27; Matthew 5:9

1. **There is the peace people can *fake*.**
"They have misled my people, saying 'Peace,' when there is no peace" (Ezekiel 13:10).

2. **There is peace people can *take*.**
"Peace I leave with you; my peace I give to you; not as the world gives do I give to you" (John 14:27).

3. **There is the peace people can *make*.**
"Blessed are the peacemakers, for they shall be called sons of God" (Matthew 5:9).

HOW GOD PLANS TO MAKE MEN HOLY

Do this, and you will live. Luke 10:28 *Christ [left] you an example, that you should follow in his steps.* 1 Peter 2:21 *If any man would come after me, let him deny himself and take up his cross and follow Me.* Matthew 16:24

135

Lo, I am with you always, to the close of the age. Matthew 28:20 *God who knows the heart bore witness to them, giving them the Holy Spirit just as he did to us; and he made no distinction between us and them, but cleansed their hearts by faith.* Acts 15:8,9 *When he appears we shall be like him, for we shall see him as he is.* 1 John 3:2

All Christians believe that it is God's intention to take His people to heaven at last, but heaven is the home of the holy. "Nothing unclean shall enter it" (Revelation 21:27). To take them to heaven, therefore, God must first make them holy, for they cannot make themselves holy.

Precisely *how* does God propose to do it? Different theories prevail.

    a. Some say that we can never be holy in this life.

    b. Some say that God can make us holy at one stroke.

    c. Some say that holiness can be produced only by a prolonged process.

What is the right view? It will emerge as we examine the relevant passages of Scripture listed above.

God has six ways of doing it.

1. The commands of a code.

2. The excellence of an example.

3. The constraints of a cross.

4. The challenge of a companionship.

5. The inspiration of an indwelling.

6. The splendor of a spectacle.

LIKE A TREE

He is like a tree. Psalm 1:3

Someone once said that although James Denney, the distinguished Scottish theologian, was a man of fine and firm character, you would as soon think of putting your arm through his as you would of twining it round the branch of an oak. Denney was like a tree in one sense, but not in another. This botanical figure of the Psalmist's suggests three things about the righteous person he is describing.

It hints that he is:

1. **Like a tree in stability.**

2. **Like a tree in virility.**

3. **Like a tree in longevity.**

It is not growing like a tree
In bulk, doth make men better be;
Or standing long an oak, three hundred year,
To fall a log at last, dry, bald, and sere;
　　A lily of a day
　　Is fairer far in May,
Although it fall and die that night,
It was the plant and flower of light.
In small proportions we just beauties see;
And in short measures, life may perfect be.

　　　　　　　　　　　　　　　Ben Jonson

That is true. And yet, according to the Old Testament, longevity is one of the tokens of the Lord's favor.

The Practicality of Christ

Luke 13:23,24;   Acts 1:6-8;   John 21:22

Undiscerning critics sometimes airily dismiss Jesus Christ as a spiritual dreamer, an impractical poetic sort of person whose philosophy of life is idealistic, and unrelated to the hard facts of this workaday world.

Nothing could be further from the truth. Jesus was in fact extremely practical. I say nothing about His being a carpenter, and so habituated to handling material things. In spiritual matters, too, He was extremely and extraordinarily practical.

Three examples:

1. **To the speculative question, "Lord, will those who are saved be few?" He replied with the practical directive, "Strive to enter by the narrow door; for many, I tell you, will seek to enter and will not be able"** (Luke 13:23,24).

2. **To the speculative query, "Lord, will you at this time restore the kingdom to Israel?" He replied with the practical prediction, "You shall receive power when the Holy Spirit has come upon you"** (Acts 1:6, 8).

3. **To the speculative inquiry, "Lord, what about this man?" Jesus responded with the practical command, "Follow me!"** (John 21:22).

A RELIGION FOR MIDNIGHT

Which of you who has a friend will go to him at midnight and say to him, "Friend, lend me three loaves." Luke 11:5 *About midnight Paul and Silas were . . . singing hymns to God.* Acts 16:25 *Paul . . . prolonged his speech until midnight.* Acts 20:7

"Christianity," wrote William Robertson Nicoll, "is a religion for midnight." It is indeed. If any form of faith is not a religion for midnight it is not fit to be a religion at all. Our texts teach us that Christians do three things at midnight.

1. **At midnight they go to their divine Friend.**

Only heaven is sweeter than to talk with Christ at midnight.

2. **At midnight they sing to their divine Friend.**

"Where is God my Maker, who gives songs in the night?" (Job 35:10).

3. **At midnight they listen to the voice of their divine Friend.**

For some years I lived in the heart of London almost within sight of Big Ben, the huge clock at the top of the tower surmounting the Houses of Parliament which tolls out the hours with its iron tongue. Through the day, because of the noise of the traffic, I could not hear from my home the booming of the bell, but at night in the hush of the dark, it could be heard distinctly. Midnight is the time to listen.

139

CHRIST AND BREAD

The bread which we break. 1 Corinthians 10:16

Consider six striking points of analogy between Christ and bread.

1. The burying.

"Truly, truly, I say to you, unless a grain of wheat falls into the earth and dies, it remains alone; but if it dies, it bears much fruit" (John 12:24).

2. The bruising.

"He was bruised for our iniquities. . . . it was the will of the Lord to bruise Him" (Isaiah 53:5,10).

3. The baking.

At Calvary Christ passed through the fire of God's righteous anger against sin.

4. The blessing.

"He took the bread and blessed, and broke it, and gave it to them" (Luke 24:30).

5. The breaking.

"The Lord Jesus . . . took bread, and when He had given thanks, he broke it" (1 Corinthians 11:23,24).

6. The buying.

"How are we to buy bread, so that these people may eat?" (John 6:5).

If we are to have the Bread of Life, we shall have to be willing to pay the price.

The Symphony of Communal Prayer

If two of you agree on earth about anything they ask, it will be done for them by my Father in heaven. (Matthew 18:19)

The word translated *agree* in our text is very interesting. In Greek it is *sumphonesosin,* a term from which, by almost exact transliteration, we get our word *symphony.*

What is needed to produce a symphony?

1. **A composer.**

It is the Spirit who is the true source of prayer.

2. **A theme.**

It is the Spirit who prompts true prayer. "The Spirit helps us in our weakness; for we do not know how to pray as we ought, but the Spirit himself intercedes for us with sighs too deep for words" (Romans 8:26).

3. **Performers.**

Those who meet to pray.

4. **A conductor.**

Christ must be the musical director.

5. **It is usual to have an audience.**

Every prayer meeting is a Royal Command Performance. The King Himself is present, and it is to Him primarily that the music is addressed, but others also are permitted to hear it. "Since we are surrounded by so great a cloud of witnesses, let us . . . [look] to Jesus . . . who

. . . is seated at the right hand of the throne of God"
(Hebrews 12:1,2).

The Son of Man—Eating and Drinking
A Communion Sermon Outline

The Son of man came eating and drinking. Matthew 11:19
*The Lord Jesus on the night when he was betrayed took
bread, and when he had given thanks, he broke it, and
said, "This is my body which is for you." . . . In the same
way also the cup, after supper, saying, "This cup is the
new covenant in my blood. Do this, as often as you drink
it, in remembrance of me.* 1 Corinthians 11:23-25 [We]
ate and drank with him after he rose from the dead. Acts
10:41

Unlike that of His great contemporary, John the Baptist,
the life of Christ—if we except the forty days of fasting
in the desert—was not marked by the austerity of dietetic
asceticism. He came eating and drinking.

1. **He came into history eating and drinking.**
That was proof of His real humanity.

2. **He came to the Holy Table eating and drinking.**
That was a symbol of mystical communion.

3. **He came from Hades still eating and drinking.**
That was a demonstration of the fact that He rose
bodily from the dead.

The Speaking Dead

A Funeral Sermon

He being dead yet speaketh. Hebrews 11:4, KJV

Not long ago I had a most memorable experience. Sitting in the lounge of the home of a friend of mine, a professor of astrophysics in Berkeley University, California, I was listening to a record of readings of his own poems made by Dylan Thomas.

Hearing the poet's musical voice, I remembered standing by the little wooden cross surmounting his grave in the churchyard at Laugharne, in South Wales. Into my mind flashed the text: "He being dead yet speaketh."

1. **The dead speak to the consciences of the living by their remembered pattern of behavior.**

2. **The dead in some cases speak to the wills of the living by the challenge of their great achievements.**

3. **The dead speak to the hearts of the living by the tender recollections they evoke.**

The Armor of Light

Let us . . . put on the armor of light. Romans 13:12

How irrelevant and obsolete in this age of the atom does armor appear! Such a collection of it as may be seen, for instance, in the Tower of London, impresses thoughtful modern people with a sense of the magnitude of the changes which have happened in human history since the days when men wore vizored helmets and corselets of steel. But there is one kind of armor which is never outdated nor unserviceable—the armor of God's light.

1. **Light is an armor against germs.**
It protects us against invasion by microbes.

2. **Light is an armor against accidents.**
Many fatalities on the roads are caused by defective lighting.

3. **Light is an armor against ignorance.**
We are so accustomed to light being available, that we often forget that we owe all our book learning to illumination, natural or artificial. The light of knowledge would not have reached us as it has without the light of nature.

THE WIND

The wind blows where it wills, and you hear the sound of it, but you do not know whence it comes or whither it goes; so it is with every one who is born of the Spirit. John 3:8

Here we have brought before us:

1. **The mystery of the wind.**
"You do not know whence it comes or whither it goes."

2. **The mastery of the wind.**
"The wind blows where it wills."

3. The melody of the wind.
"You hear the sound of it."

We have all read of the German baron who lived in a castle situated in a narrow gorge much visited by the winds, and who had wires strung across the gorge, thus forming an Aolian harp on which the breezes played brave music. So the Holy Spirit makes melody in the heart that receives Him.

AN IDEAL CHURCH

The church . . . had peace and was built up; and walking in the fear of the Lord and in the comfort of the Holy Spirit it was multiplied. Acts 9:31

An ideal church is:

1. Pacified.
"Had peace."

2. Edified.
"And was built up."

3. Sanctified.
"Walked in the fear of the Lord."

4. Fortified.
"And in the comfort of the Holy Spirit."

5. Multiplied.
"It was multiplied."

CHRIST AS BIOGRAPHER

Truly, truly, I say to you, when you were young, you girded yourself and walked where you would; but when you are old, you will stretch out your hands, and another will gird you and carry you where you do not wish to go. John 21:18

In this passage we see our Lord in a novel role, that of biographer. Here in a thumbnail sketch, He tells Peter's life story. It is a brief biography, but it is representative. "Every Christian man," said Origen, "is Peter."

There are three chapters.

1. **The independence of youth.**

"When you were young, you girded yourself and walked where you would."

2. **The infirmity of age.**

"When you are old, you will stretch out your hands, and another will gird you."

3. **The inevitability of the cross.**

"Follow me" (v.19).

THE SHEPHERD

I will strike the Shepherd, and the sheep will be scattered. Mark 14:27 *You were straying like sheep, but have now returned to the Shepherd and Guardian of your souls.*

1 Peter 2:25 *I have other sheep, that are not of this fold; I must bring them also, and they will heed my voice. So there shall be one flock, one shepherd.* John 10:16

In these texts we have brought before us:

1. **The stricken Shepherd and the scattered sheep.**
2. **The risen Shepherd and the gathered sheep.**
3. **The seeking shepherd and the folded sheep.**

FORGETTING THAT WE HAVE BEEN CLEANSED

Whoever lacks these things is blind and shortsighted and has forgotten that he was cleansed from his old sins. 2 Peter 1:9

There is a famous play in which a schoolmaster is represented as having murdered a man. After that, he could not bear to look in the faces of the innocent children. He buried the body, but had to dig it up; he plunged it in a stream, but the stream ran dry; he covered it with leaves, but the wind blew them away.

Only Christ can deal effectively with sin, and yet we Christians sometimes forget that our sin *has* been dealt with. We cease to remember that we have been cleansed from our old sins.

Many things in life we *must* forget. "Life cannot go on without much forgetting," declared Honoré de Balzac. But this we ought never to suffer to lapse from our consciousness: that our iniquities have been taken away, and our sins purged.

When we do forget this, what happens?

1. **Sometimes when we thus forget, we become complacent.**

2. **Sometimes when we thus forget, we become worried.**

3. **Sometimes when we thus forget, we become censorious of others.**

Numbered With the Transgressors

He . . . was numbered with the transgressors. Isaiah 53:12

We like to be numbered with the best people. If anybody is rich or famous or powerful or popular, we like to be seen in his company and to have our names linked with his.

Jesus was numbered with the worst people, associated in the public mind of His time with the basest and meanest of men.

1. **He was numbered with the transgressors at His baptism.**

"In those days came John the Baptist, preaching in the wilderness of Judea: 'Repent, for the kingdom of heaven is at hand.' . . . Then went out to him Jerusalem and all Judea and all the region about the Jordan, . . . confessing their sins. . . . Then Jesus came from Galilee to the Jordan to John, to be baptized by him. John would have prevented him, saying, 'I need to be baptized by you, and do you come to me?' But Jesus answered him, 'Let it be so now, for thus it is fitting for us to fulfill all righteousness' " (Matthew 3:1,6,13,14,15).

"Thus it is fitting for us." Mark that momentous *us*. It is the us of complete identification with humanity of One who in His high-priestly prayer was to use the same pronoun in a colossal context. "That they may all be one; even as thou, Father, art in me, and I in thee, that they also may be in us" (John 17:21).

Jesus could so easily have taken His stand with the Baptist over against the penitents, saying, "Come on, John, I'll help you to baptize these sinners." In His infinite humility, He didn't. He took His stand with the sinners and begged John to baptize Him. He was numbered with the transgressors at His baptism.

2. **He was numbered with the transgressors in His ministry.**

"Now the tax collectors and sinners were all drawing near to hear Him. And the Pharisees and the scribes murmured, saying: 'This Man receives sinners and eats with them' " (Luke 15:1,2).

3. **He was numbered with the transgressors on the cross.**

"And with him they crucified two robbers, one on his right and one on his left" (Mark 15:27).

What must I do? Mark 10:17

1. **Be yourself.**

2. **Give yourself.**

3. **Lose yourself.**

4. **Find yourself.**

THE SUMMING UP

Micah 6:8; 1 Corinthians 13:13

Everyone who has thought deeply about life has come, sooner or later, to certain final conclusions about it. Complexity of thought resolves itself into simplicity of thought, and in a few well-chosen words the great man gives his summing up of things.

Let us consider four consummate examples of this.

1. **The summing up of John Keats**
In his great poem "Ode on a Grecian Urn" he writes:
"Beauty is truth, truth beauty,"—that is all
Ye know on earth and all ye need to know.

2. **The summing of Alfred Tennyson**
There are two oft-quoted lines in his "Oenone" in which he crystallizes his moral philosophy:
Self-reverence, self-knowledge, self-control,
These three alone lead life to sovereign power.

3. The summing up of Micah

"What does the Lord require of you but to do justice, and to love kindness, and to walk humbly with your God?" (Micah 6:8).

4. The summing up of Paul

"So faith, hope, love abide, these three; but the greatest of these is love" (1 Corinthians 13:13).

THE HANDS OF PAUL

With my own hand. Galatians 6:11

Chrysostom, the golden-mouthed orator of the early Church, in a sermon eulogizing the great apostle to the Gentiles, breaks out dramatically, "Fain would I see the dust of those hands through which the divine writings were penned!"

Let us, in imagination, look at those hands for a moment. What are they?

1. **They are the hands of an accomplice in a judicial murder:** the red hands of the persecutor.

2. **They are the hands of a skillful and industrious tentmaker:** the rough hands of the toiler.

3. **They are the hands of a great author:** the nimble hands of the writer.

4. **They are the hands of a praying saint:** the reverent hands of the intercessor.

CHRIST STIRRING UP THE PEOPLE

He stirs up the people. Luke 23:5

These words were meant as an indictment of Jesus. They were part of a legal charge preferred against Him. They were designed by the rabble who uttered them to bring discredit on Christ and to set Him up before the Roman authorities in the hated role of revolutionary. "He stirs up the people."

Yet the sentence was true in a way of which our Lord's accusers never dreamt. Christ was, and ever is, a stirrer up of people.

During His earthly life,

1. **He stirred up the people** physically.

How many came to Him with flagging health and went away stirred to new life!

2. **He stirred up the people** morally.

See how He turned upside down the moral assessments of His time! He stirred the scribes and Pharisees to the bottom and the publicans and sinners to the top!

3. **He stirred up the people** spiritually.

FAITH THAT WORKS

Faith working through love. Galatians 5:6

There are four relations in which faith and works may

stand to one another. It will be for our spiritual profit and enlightenment to review them rapidly now.

1. **It is not faith *and* works:**
that is Romanism.

2. **It is not faith *without* works:**
that is Pietism.

3. **It is not works *without* faith:**
that is Moralism.

4. **It is faith *that* works:**
that is true Christianity, and such faith works through love.

THE REWARDS OF RIGHT DECISION

The Book of Ruth

We see four rewards of right decision in this Book of Ruth.

1. **Refuge.**
"The Lord recompense you for what you have done, and a full reward be given you by the Lord, the God of Israel, under whose wings you have come to take refuge!" (2:12).

2. **Rest.**
"My daughter, should I not seek a home for you, that it may be well with you?" (3:1).

3. Redemption.

"Ruth, the Moabitess, . . . I have bought to be my wife" (4:10).

4. Renown.

"May his name be renowned in Israel!" (4:14).

(Faris D. Whitesell, *Power in Expository Preaching* Westwood, N.J., Fleming H. Revell, 1963, p. 50.)

LAZARUS AT THE TABLE

Lazarus was one of those at table with Him. John 12:2.

Of all people, Lazarus was the last person one would have looked for at the table that day. Not long before that, he had been in a tomb, and those who occupy ledges in tombs do not occupy seats at tables. Yet Lazarus was there.

Was there not a time in our experience when it would have seemed almost as unlikely that we, then dead in trespasses and sins, would be found sitting at the sacramental table as we are today? Yet here we are!

1. Lazarus was at the table because he had been raised to life by Christ.

We are here for the same reason. As Paul puts it in his Letter to the Ephesians: "And you he made alive, when you were dead through the trespasses and sins in which you once walked, following the course of this world, following the prince of the power of the air, the spirit that is now at work in the sons of disobedience" (Ephesians 2:1,2).

2. Lazarus was at the table because he was loved by Christ.

So are we! "See what love the Father has given us, that we should be called children of God; and so we are. The reason why the world does not know us is that it did not know him. Beloved, we are God's children now; it does not yet appear what we shall be, but we know that when he appears we shall be like him, for we shall see him as he is" (1 John 3:1,2).

3. Lazarus was at the table because he was loosed by Christ.

So are we! Life that lacks liberty is hardly life at all. Christ not only quickens, He frees us. "You will know the truth, and the truth will make you free. . . . If the Son makes you free, you will be free indeed" (John 8:32,36).

THE STRONG TOWER

The name of the Lord is a strong tower; the righteous man runs into it and is safe. Proverbs 18:10

In the British Museum, London, there is a medal struck to commemorate the jubilee of the promulgation of the Confession of Augsburg. This famous Confession is a statement of Protestant belief drawn up by Philip Melanchthon under the personal supervision of Martin Luther. On its reverse side, the medal bears the Latin inscription: *Turris fortissima nomen Domini,* "The name of the Lord is a strong tower."

1. Think of the inward security of the tower.

2. Think of the upward reach of the tower.

3. Think of the outward vision from the tower.

LAMPS OF THE LORD

Let your light so shine before men, that they may see your good works and give glory to your Father who is in heaven. Matthew 5:16

1. **Lamps must be lit.**
They cannot light themselves. Someone must kindle them.

2. **Lamps must be fed.**
If deprived of fuel, they cannot continue to shine.

3. **Lamps must be trimmed.**
There is always the possibility that the flame may burn low or even go out because the wick is not clean.

4. **Lamps must be placed.**
Jesus makes a special point of this. It is of no use to put a lamp under a bushel, or under a bed but in a candlestick or lampstand, so that it may give illumination to all in the house.

BUT HE FORGOT
A COMMUNION SERMON OUTLINE

"Remember me, when it is well with you." Yet the

chief butler did not remember Joseph, but forgot him. Genesis 40:14,23

Remember me. That has been the pathetic, poignant cry of the human heart in all ages. Remember me. It is the soul's protest against oblivion, the self's agonized appeal against utter ultimate forgottenness. Remember me. That was the cry of the Pharaohs, the ancient rulers of Egypt. That was the cry, too, of Christina Rossetti. In her poem "Remember," she writes touchingly:

> Remember me when I am gone away,
>> Gone far away into the silent land;
> When you can no more hold me by the hand,
>> Nor I half turn to go, yet turning stay;
> Remember me when no more, day by day,
>> You tell me of our future that you planned:
> Only remember me. . . .

That was the cry of Joseph when, having interpreted the chief butler's dream and foretold his re-establishment in royal favor, he ventured to put in for himself the deeply moving plea, "Remember me when it is well with you."

1. He had been requested to remember, but he forgot. We, too, have been requested to remember. Do *we* forget?

James T. Cleland writes: "My own mother loved the Lord's Supper. For over sixty years she almost never missed a celebration. She prepared herself for it with care. I sought her interpretation of the Lord's Supper. She looked at me frankly and said, 'Our Lord asked His friends

157

not to forget Him. I am one of His friends. I do not forget Him.'" (*Wherefore Art Thou Come?* New York & Nashville, Abingdon Press, 1961, p. 30.)

2. He had reason to remember, but he forgot.
We also have reason to remember. Do *we* forget?

A young woman came up to Dr. H. A. Ironside at the close of an address and said: "I do not like the way you put things. You made me feel very uncomfortable tonight. I have never knowingly done a wicked thing. I am respected by all my friends. No one can say a word against my character. The only thing that you yourself could object to is that I do not belong to any church, or care anything about Jesus Christ; and yet you class me with people who are living wickedly." He replied, "Suppose you came and told me something like this: I have always been good and respectable. Nobody can say anything against me except that, although I have the best mother in the world, I do not care anything about her. I am utterly indifferent to her. What would you expect me to think of you?" "O," she exclaimed, "I could not be a good girl and not love my mother!" "Well," he went on, "I told you tonight of One who has loved you with a love such as no earthly mother ever knew; One who for your sake gave His life to ransom you from a danger which your finite mind cannot realize and who now asks your trust and confidence, and you boldly say you care nothing about Him! What do you suppose God thinks of such indifference to His Son?" She hung her head and said, "I never thought of it like that!" And a few nights later she humbly confessed the Lord Jesus Christ as her own Saviour. (J. Oswald Sanders, *The Holy Spirit of Promise*, London, Marshall, Morgan & Scott, 1959, p. 49.)

The chief butler had reason not only to remember Joseph because of the past, but also because of the future. Joseph was to be prime minister of Egypt one day.

3. **His recollection was stimulated, and he remembered that he had forgotten.**

"I remember my faults today" (Genesis 41:9).

By the sight of the holy table and its sacramental symbols our memories too are stirred, and we gratefully recall what Jesus has done for us.

> According to Thy gracious word,
>   In meek humility,
> This will I do, my dying Lord,
>   I will remember Thee.
> Thy body, broken for my sake,
>   My bread from heaven shall be;
> Thy testamental cup I take,
>   And thus remember Thee.
> And when these failing lips grow dumb,
>   And mind and memory flee,
> When Thou shalt in Thy kingdom come,
>   Then, Lord, remember me.
>   James Montgomery